For George and Garrick —
my true friends and kindred
spirits —

      Love,

          Kati

          April 1987

AN AMERICAN WOMAN

Also by Kati Marton: *Wallenberg*

An American Woman

A NOVEL BY

Kati Marton

W · W · NORTON & COMPANY

NEW YORK · LONDON

First Edition

The text of this book is composed in Janson Alternate, with display type set in
Delphin No. 1. Composition and manufacturing by the Haddon Craftsmen, Inc.
Book design by Marjorie J. Flock.

Library of Congress Cataloging-in-Publication Data

Marton, Kati.
An American woman.

I. Title.
PS3563.A739A8   1987   813'.54   86-16342

ISBN 0-393-02420-2

W. W. Norton & Company, Inc., 500 Fifth Avenue, New York, N. Y. 10110
W. W. Norton & Company Ltd., 37 Great Russell Street, London WC1B 3NU

1 2 3 4 5 6 7 8 9 0

FOR PETER

AN AMERICAN WOMAN

Just because it's already happened does not mean the past is finished.
—*Kundera*

One

THE HEAVY STEEL DOOR shut behind her. I have been here before, she thought. And, for just a moment, this vague familiarity softened the sound of the steel door's bolt slide into place. My God, her mother had not embellished the truth. The place was dimmer and felt more subterranean than any cellar she had ever been in. And no cellar was this small nor had such a heavy door, without even a keyhole on the inside. And a quiet that had nothing to do with this world.

Anna Bator touched her forehead to the rough, damp cinderblock wall to remind herself she was not dreaming. The cold and a sudden realization jolted her. She was an inmate of the Fo Street Maximum Security Prison, on the Left Bank of the Danube in Budapest. Two decades earlier, her parents had been prisoners here.

The adrenalin which had sustained her during her arrest and its bureaucratic aftermath had begun to ebb. Her arms and legs felt soft and limp. But the tight little cot, with its filthy gray blanket, no, she was not yet ready to sit on that.

She would stay on her feet as long as possible. She walked six careful steps from end to end. People, it occurred to her, spent entire mornings, afternoons, and nights in this cell. Weeks and months and years. How, she wondered.

It was June and Anna wore a light silk blouse. A sea green silk suitable for early June in Budapest. But not for the chilly, fetid air of a cell. The blouse stuck in clammy patches under her arms and against her back. She had been wearing a great deal of silk ever since Christopher Shepherd told her he liked touching her in silk. She was cold now and very tired.

At last, Anna dropped heavily on the cot. Jesus, it happens so fast, she thought. This transformation from a member of the human race into an outsider, a prisoner. Years before, as she lay staring at the ceiling of the recovery room, spent from Sarah's hard birth, she had a foretaste of this. She had wondered, then, if she would ever again be like everybody else. Able to walk, laugh, and be annoyed by traffic and the rain.

She reached for the blanket finally. Though it smelled sour, she draped it like a shawl around her shoulders. Already she was becoming less squeamish. Becoming a prisoner?

Anna buried her nose in the crook of her arm, sniffing deeply a faint trace of Chanel No. 5 still on her blouse. How many women (perhaps her mother among them) had resorted to this trick to momentarily soothe their nostrils from the rancid smell of urine? She tried to avoid looking at the open toilet, just behind the cot.

It was all still happening to someone else. Her arrest, swift and undramatic, and now this surreal house of horrors:

the drab set of a low-budget film. So far she had performed
like an actress. The memory of other tight spots helped. The
hours spent driving around Damascus with a listless PLO
"artillery expert" who gripped the steering wheel with one
hand and a Kalashnikov with the other. But she was not in
the Middle East now. Nor in Nicaragua. She was in her own
country. The place of her birth. Her arrest felt quite personal: the final scene of a family drama.

Anna's was not another phony arrest, calculated by the
Party's appetite for a random dose of terror, to remind the
people this was still a totalitarian state. And don't be fooled
by the presence of a Hilton, a Hyatt House, and (so it was
rumored) soon a Burger Chef.

Her former homeland was hailed for its cheerful face in
the West. ("What a marvelous time we had in Budapest!"
she often heard around dinner tables in Washington and
New York. "It's simply not possible to have a bad meal, you
know.") Anna, however, had recently relearned what she
had known as a child: that fear and unquestioned authority
were the stilts which propped up this New Socialism. In
another, earlier life, she had come by this insight the way
other children learn to stay in their rooms when their parents' voices take on a certain edge. The hard way. But quite
by chance.

Gradually, in the way a patient accepts anesthesia, she
gave in to the almost soothing inevitability of prison. She
had been seeking for so long, prison was a way station at
least. She was convinced this would be a temporary stop.

So, she sat now on the narrow cot, felt its springs dig
into her thighs, but she didn't feel the suffocating panic a
real prisoner must feel. She still felt like a visitor. An ob-

server. Two decades of living in America, half that time
spent as a journalist, had bred that feeling of immunity.
Anna's fear at this early stage was something soft and mallea-
ble.

She found the cell's permanent twilight conducive to
thought. It was like a dimmed theater waiting for actors and
stage sets. Certain details started floating back from her
memory's archives. "The moment you take a step toward
the toilet," she recalled her mother saying, "the eye in the
Judas is on you. Another step in the prisoner's prescribed
degradation," Julia Bator had told her, her mother's small,
pale hands flicking this notion away as ridiculous when
attached to herself.

Her mother's descriptions. Her mother's memories of
prison. Like the wives of criminals or spies who assume the
habit of silence, her mother had been talking for two for as
long as Anna could remember. It seemed to Anna as if
emotions and memories were too exhausting for her father.
He let his wife fill the void with her stream of recollections,
while he withdrew into a place of his own.

Anna punched a tight fist against the rough cinderblock.
The smugness of the man. What gave him the right to grip
his long cigarette between thin lips and contain the humiliation and the mystery of all that took place before her birth
in one look of gray rectitude? That's why she sat now in this
damn hole.

She had not been able to simply ease him out of her
consciousness and get on with life, the way she had seen her
friends sweep their parents out of theirs. Nor could she turn
visits home into annual acts of charity, like sending a check
to the United Fund. Anna had seen too much. She had seen

her father's jaw go slack at the sight of dark-suited messengers closing in on him. Seen him as a sagging old man of forty in the courtyard of the Supreme Court, moments before they pronounced him traitor. There were other images which she could not erase. Newer images (for her), but dating from before her birth. Her father already wearing a death mask as he voluntarily clambered aboard the airless train, careful to avoid contact with either guards or fellow captives. Was that when he developed his habit of never looking straight at you?

The anger, a burn in her chest, passed. It always did when she recalled these things. War wounds can take many forms, she thought. A man found frozen in Lafayette Park across the street from the White House, his feet wrapped in newspapers, turns out to be a thrice-decorated hero of the Tet Offensive; the victim of war wounds that did not heal in civilian life. A man who does not make a friend for thirty-five, forty years, who is afraid to tell his own child how he got here, and who does not look people directly in the eye, ever, is also a victim of war wounds.

Yes, but I too have memories that had no place to go but back here, where it all began. She could not live the fresh, flat life her father stage-managed for her. Maybe you were too shell-shocked from your wounds for anything else. Your soul may have died in Budapest, but mine has not. And, again, her resentment gathered strength, broke over her like a wave. Impotent, prison anger, she thought. She must think of something else.

Idly, she started composing the *Evening News* script of her arrest. "United News Service foreign correspondent Anna Bator, an American citizen, has been taken into Hun-

garian police custody tonight." Everything was always "tonight" on the broadcast. Never mind the actual time of her
arrest. "Tonight" gave it an air of urgency, made the viewer
feel as though this were a really hot item. She could visualize
Jim McGuire, who filled the small screen, if not real space,
with magnificent shoulders, stentorian voice aching with
concern, his silver head not in the least upstaged by Anna's
grainy photograph peering over his left shoulder. "Ms. Bator," McGuire would read off the Teleprompter, "has been
in the Hungarian capital to set up UNS's first permanent
Eastern Bloc bureau. Both UNS and the State Department
have protested this blatant infringement of the Helsinki Ac-
cords by the Hungarian government and have called for the
immediate release of the Hungarian-born broadcaster."

Depending on how many fatalities resulted from the
latest Gush Emunim groundbreaking on the West Bank, or
whether Teddy Kennedy chose "tonight" to confirm wide-
spread rumors of his upcoming engagement to a blonde and
nubile member of the U.S. Olympic Ski Team, McGuire
might or might not devote thirty more seconds to Anna's
rather unorthodox (in the world of network news) background. The truth was she didn't give a damn any longer.

Anna had this over the other new inmates of the Fo
Street: she knew the house rules. Some parents spellbind
their children with tales of how they once crossed the Negev
on camelback or floated down the white waters of some
turbulent African river in a raft. Anna's mother had hypnotized her with details of their imprisonment. Not because she
was trying to impress Anna, but primarily because this was
a piece of her parents' past which they deemed to be a
subject suitable for recounting. A heroic chapter: in the
mid-fifties, during the final kick of Stalinism, her mother

and father had been arrested, tried, and convicted as American spies. Their "crime" had been their work as correspondents for an American news magazine. In those days, for a Hungarian to work for a Western organization (particularly a news service) was tantamount to signing on with the enemy.

"I had picked my 'uniform' with care." Julia Bator smiled a conqueror's smile when she regaled her child with this. "A full tartan skirt that covered me like a tent. The guards couldn't see a thing when they peered through the Judas."

Anna touched her face, realized it had been hours since she had seen her own reflection. And wouldn't for how long? "I used the bottom of my tin cup as a mirror," her mother had said. "It was not exactly a clear image, but that was just as well. Prison," Julia said, a light finger skimming her immaculately groomed brow, "makes you ugly."

Ugly was not a word anyone had ever used to describe Anna. Its prospect, even now, did not register as a threat. At thirty-six, she had just reached her prime, and she knew it. Her body was leaner, more mobile, and certainly more self-aware than in her twenties. Her face had lost all traces of the softness that had once given her features a look of compliant sweetness. It was a face now dominated by oversized hazel eyes, eyes that no longer sought to please so much as to observe and record. Anna frankly liked her looks and regretted not being able to see her own image, much as she would miss seeing a valued friend for a time.

"Humor," her mother had said. "That I never lost. Even during interrogation. I would tell the Major he could only have my confession in exchange for a shampoo and set."

Remembering this, Anna had tried a bit of humor with the secret policeman who served as her arresting officer.

"This is no worse than renewing my New York State driver's license," she had said to him as he pressed her fingers, one by one, on the inkpad. The sandy-haired colonel permitted his lips to shift into a half smile that may only have been a facial tic. The secret policeman had a pot of pink geraniums on his windowsill, a dazzling and reproachful burst of life in the hard, gray room. The agent looked too young to be performing a task of such numbing boredom. Why wasn't he outside, putting those large hands to good use? He avoided her eyes, which sought his.

There was something about his features, the cleft chin, innocently upturned nose, and watery gray eyes, that struck her as familiar. Beneath the jowls, the features gone soft, the red-rimmed eyes, she saw a boy. Berci. Berci Toth. Yes. "I'll follow you," he had threatened, age fourteen and hopelessly smitten. "All the way to Vienna, if you leave. I'll find you, Anna. I promise." She had walked away. She was ten years old and embarrassed by his passion. For a while she had kept an eye out for him in Vienna. His declaration of endless love meant something, after all. But she never saw him. Until today?

Her first conquest. She avoided his eyes now, embarrassed for both of them. But it calmed her, this recognition of a childhood face. For Berci, if it was Berci, whose heart had once ached for her, she feigned composure. She checked the flood of questions that burned for answers. In their own time, her father had told her once, your interrogators tell you the full list of charges against you. What she now had was a number and time to think.

Too busy searching Berci's features for her childhood sweetheart, she had forgotten to ask him about the invasion. How would she find out now if the Warsaw Pact armies had carried out their planned occupation of Poland? In this newsless world, she would never know.

She was beginning to lose track of the hour. Her watch, rings, and gold chains, along with her small blue American passport, were all filed inside Berci's steel cabinet. The meager stream of gray light the small window filtered in was no help in telling time.

Her father had once told her the quiet was intended to make the prisoner concentrate on his crimes. Not that Alex or Julia Bator had ever imagined their little girl would follow them there. They had transported her halfway around the world, raised her a proud citizen of the United States of America. They thought they had slammed and locked the door on what they left behind.

It turned out to have been a naive dream. Anna did not want the past to be finished. She was haunted by it. Everybody had a history, knew what their grandparents looked liked and whether they had died peacefully in their beds, in the company of loved ones, or otherwise. Anna had only recently gathered these simple facts about her own family, but the facts were cold, without the flesh and blood of shared human emotions. Only her father could have breathed life into them, and he refused to do so.

So she had come back out of need. She knew what it would do to him, the thought of Anna sitting on a cot in a cell in the Fo Street. But he had hurt her too much with his impenetrable composure.

Shepherd . . . She would put off thoughts of Shepherd. Postpone needing him as long as possible. At any rate, he seemed worlds removed from her dark cell. Anna had needed a man, briefly and acutely, at every stage in her life. This was different, she felt sure. She was putting aside other

childish habits as well. Illusions. Yesterday's dreams. One
thing was certain, Shepherd would have been appalled at
how meekly she had followed the three plainclothesmen
who had knocked at her hotel door.

She had not protested: "I'm an American citizen. I am
here as a journalist. Accredited by your government." None
of that. She had been expecting them, waiting for them, in
a way. In part because she recalled a similar knock, and
similar impassive faces, a quarter of a century earlier.

The memory of her mother's arrest never left her. She
had also witnessed her father's abduction, but that had not
left the same residue: the bitter taste of complicity with her
mother's jailers. (Guilt, too, because her father had been her
life's real preoccupation.)

Suddenly, an unexpected ripple of children's laughter
from a nearby playground hit her like a slap. She recalled her
mother saying that had been the most painful part of her
own imprisonment: to hear the laughter of children, never
your own. What a stroke of genius on the part of the AVO,
Hungary's secret police, to have built a playground less than
a block from the prison. How better to wear down a
mother's or father's final layer of resistance than to expose
them daily to the shouts and cries of children?

How long, Anna wondered, before Sarah begins to really miss me? Or before she herself would be overwhelmed
by the need to hold that unkempt blond head and sniff that
blend of bubble gum and peanut butter which was her rare
perfume? What if Sarah begins *not* to miss me? Anna had
been only a few years older than Sarah when she opened the
door to face her own mother's jailers.

Two

THE LITTLE GIRL was cocooned in a six-year-old's perfect self-centeredness the year they arrested her parents. She was a coquette fully aware of her charms. Strangers had been stopping her on the street since she was a baby. ("Those big eyes!" "May we take her picture?" they sometimes asked her parents, who pretended not to enjoy the fuss.) Anna was an only child, accustomed to her parents' near total attention. The possibility that someday her mother and father would not be there for her was simply not imaginable.

"Is it really all right to cut this up?" her playmate Zsuzsi asked that morning, eyes wide with wonder. "It's so beautiful," she said, reverently stroking the white chiffon with its oversize green polka dots, Anna's mother's cast-off. "Sure." Anna shrugged. "Nobody wears these big skirts anymore . . . not . . . you know . . . out there . . . in the West." Anna explained haltingly, for her friend Zsuzsi was from another world, a world without fashion or style; where the only thing that changed from year to year was the length of the line waiting for State Store overcoats or shoes. Zsuzsi was a True Believer, the daughter of True Believer parents. Anna admired the stark simplicity of the whole family. She was vaguely ashamed of her own mother's white-and-green-chiffon frivolity, the decadent reminder of another world, which persisted only beyond the barbed wire "out there." Anna's mother and father loved that other world and followed its tastes and fashions with religious zeal.

Three insistent knocks on the Bators' front door interrupted Anna and Zsuzsi's play. "Mommy will get it." Anna gestured in the direction of her mother's voice as she chatted on the telephone, seeping in from behind the closed door of her parent's bedroom. "Of course, darling," the girls heard Julia Bator's lilting, theatrical English. "I will be there. Alex would want it that way." Three even more determined knocks sounded from the front hall.

Anna cleared her throat. Her relationship with her mother had taken on a heated intensity since her father's arrest some weeks earlier. They were two women deprived of the man who had been their center of gravity. Willy-nilly, they were now totally dependent on each other. (Later, Anna thought her mother may well have suspected this was to be her last telephone conversation for a long time. In fact she thought her mother's proceeding in the same confident tone while her enemies were literally at her doorstep was an act of great courage, like an actress who does not miss a single line despite full knowledge of a hemorrhage beneath her costume.)

Anna did not often have the company of Zsuzsi all to herself. Zsuzsi was older, smarter, and more serious than Anna, and could easily lose interest and walk out on her.

Zsuzsi's family lived across the hall from the Bators. Anna suspected they did not approve of hers. "Your apartment looks so much more *modern* than ours," Anna had told her friend during her first visit. "So much brighter and more . . . you know . . . progressive." Was that the right word? Anna had never seen such enormous portraits of the founding fathers in a private home before, only in the post office and at school. She was impressed by the stern simplicity of Zsuzsi's mother, so different from her own.

Zsuzsi continued snipping away at Julia Bator's old dress, her large cow eyes now fixed on Anna. It was amazing what application the older girl brought to this task. Anna imagined such a thing to be well beneath Zsuzsi, who could talk in complete sentences about the Five Year Plan and the need to eliminate bourgeois influences from daily life. And when she talked about Stalin, it was as though he were her favorite uncle. With those big eyes fixed expectantly on her, Anna could hardly continue to ignore the insistent knocking on the front door.

It was not until long after her mother's arrest that Anna learned the real motive behind Zsuzsi's demonstrated passion for dolls' clothes that day. Zsuzsi's father, as serious and soft-spoken as his daughter, was, Anna learned, a lieutenant in the AVO. Father and daughter had collaborated in the smooth execution of Anna's mother's arrest.

The pounding on the door was growing louder. "Okay, okay," Anna muttered as she picked the chiffon bits off her gray, pleated skirt and stumbled irritably down the long dark corridor that led from her room to the front hall.

On her way, she closed the double glass doors that led to the living room. Why hadn't her mother done something

about those armchairs with their gaping wounds, reminders
of the night they took her father. The tufts of scratchy gray
horsehair were ugly and painful to sit on. Mother and daughter together had worked all day one Sunday a few weeks
before, replacing the books which the searchers had flung
from their shelves in a heap on the floor. Anna reluctantly
gave her stuffed rocking horse, fatally stabbed during the
same terrible night, to the concierge's daughter, Magdi.
Magdi didn't seem to even notice the animal's sad shape.
Anna did not want any reminders of that frenzied search,
when four men and a woman turned her home into a trash
heap of useless objects. They had worked so fast.

Anna had seen it all: seen them grab him on the street
in front of their house. No. She was not going to think about
that anymore. Maybe it would turn out to have been a dream
after all. Maybe she would still wake up and he would be
sitting in that straightbacked cane chair with the carved
lion's feet, the brocade upholstery smooth and shiny, without any stuffing poking out of it; sitting there listening to
Lotte Lehman on the hi-fi, the score of *Der Rosenkavalier* in
his lap.

Anna opened the door to face them. Four tall, square
figures in surprisingly clean workers' overalls. The little girl
knew. She could tell from their eyes, as dead as fish eyes,
which already looked past her into the dark apartment.
"Your mother rang about the meter," one of them lied.

A child growing up in that part of the world learns some
things very early. A faint inner voice told Anna to shout and
scream and put on the kind of hysterical display these calm
messengers of doom must despise. But at the age of six,
Anna already had a sense that arrests must be accomplished

with a minimum of fuss. People you would see waiting for the tram the day before, no longer there the next morning. And you must not shout or scream, not even if it's your own father or mother who has vanished without a trace.

She had not shouted or screamed when she saw them take her father. Her mouth had gone dry, incapable of producing a sound above a squeak. But now, they had come for her mother. The child again felt herself go as limp as a rag doll, too stunned for a bold move or even hysterics. In her self-absorbed, child's core she did not believe anyone, not even the State, could really remove her mother from her life. Her mother belonged to Anna, not to them.

And yet Anna could see that her mother and father were as out of place in this austere landscape as a pair of amaryllis plants in a muddy field. For some reason, her parents seemed to like it that way. While everyone around them whispered, they spoke in clear voices, which sounded like shouting. "Who can wear those cardboard shoes?" her father would sneer, passing a State Store window. "You're better off wrapping your feet in newspapers, then at least you don't feel cheated when they fall apart after the first rain." Her father's shoes were air-freighted from London twice a year, still in their Church's boxes, compliments of a British diplomat. Her parents seemed to follow a different set of rules from everybody else. They were so much brighter and more confident than other people. Anna felt sure they would outsmart the whole bleak system.

The child felt squeezed between the two worlds: her parents' world and the one outside. Outside, everything was makeshift and drab. Everything carried a message. Nothing was ever done without a purpose.

One day Anna's first-grade teacher asked everyone in class to bring in his favorite toy. She produced her most treasured possession: a wind-up monkey that danced a little jig while it beat on its drum. The kids in class dropped down on all fours to watch Anna's monkey perform. "Where'd you get that?" they asked, entranced by the monkey's she-nanigans. Anna, who knew the monkey was the gift of an American reporter, a colleague of her father's, knew better than to say.

Helpless, she watched the teacher leave the classroom carrying her toy monkey, suddenly transformed into an object of suspicion. "The principal would like to speak to your parents," Comrade Barna announced when she re-turned. The other children looked at Anna with expressions that blended "serves you right" with the vaguest trace of sympathy.

So the teacher wasn't interested in their toys at all. This was her own imaginative way of finding out who in the class still had ties to the "outside." For in 1954, the only toys you could find in Hungary were rough, stuffed animals no child would want to cuddle.

Anna was at once proud of the endless supply of saddle shoes and nylon blouses, and embarrassed by the flashy display of Western gifts. She felt sly when she kept quiet about those gifts, or like a show-off when she explained their origins. But even when she marched in a May Day parade with her Young Pioneer's troop, all of them turned out in regulation white shirts, dark blue trousers or pleated skirts and red kerchiefs, Anna stood out. Anna wore black patent leather shoes with a strap over the instep, from some far-off department store: Mary Janes. "Little Princess!" her playmates, resentful and envious, taunted her. There were times when she just wanted to be like everybody else.

Now Anna walked through their cluttered living room, bursting with an overaccumulation of books, mutilated armchairs, and the hastily replaced bibelots, to her mother's room. Every surface of the drafty salon she crossed was covered with china and silver boxes and figurines.

None of the dark oil paintings on the walls carried a message of any sort. They were aimless landscapes or portraits of people who did not look as though they despised the old way of doing things. By now, Anna knew that old things, foreign things, were suspect. You were meant only to look forward, and to hate the past.

Zsuzsi's apartment had such a clean, Spartan feeling. Zsuzsi's mother never wore a speck of makeup and spoke only in Hungarian. Anna secretly felt she was far better suited for both motherhood and the New Hungary than her own mother, who was still on the telephone. "Yes, a wide-brimmed picture hat would be just right," she said, winding up her conversation. "Mommy," Anna stuck her head in the door, "it's for you. The front door." Anna was already back in her own room, back under Zsuzsi's unblinking gaze and the chiffon scraps. She heard her mother's silky glide and whiffed the cloud of Arpège. Maybe, she thought, they really did come about the meter. Besides, she didn't want to embarrass Zsuzsi. So she resisted the temptation to run after her mother. To scream "No!" or just throw her arms around her mother's neck. She continued cutting up her discarded dress.

Years later, she would think, after all I was just a child, fresh from warm infancy. Only the year before, she had been roused from sleep in the dead of night on Christmas Eve by the sound of hammering. She cracked the double doors of the living room to find, not Santa Claus, but her father. His face was a web of lines of concentration as he tried to decipher the language of the American do-it-yourself kit, as foreign to him as Urdu. The end of one illusion. Really she had been just a child.

Anna did not start crying until after Zsuzsi left and she found herself alone in the quiet apartment.

The next time she saw her mother was in court during her trial.

Three

ON A DAMP December morning in 1986, she stood on the riverbank and felt as though she had never left. She had merely dreamt of other places, other people. It seemed to her as if, all along, she had walked beside the Danube and had kept to the slower rhythms of this city, untroubled by ambitions other than to live here.

The smell of the river made her throat feel tight. All her life, Anna had lived near a river: the East River, the Thames. This river exhaled the pungent blend of the grease and smoke of barge traffic and the nutlike smell of the horse chestnut trees that lined it. This river reeked of her childhood.

She faced a ragged skyline uninterrupted by any of the cold protrusions that pass for modern architecture. Budapest is a city of peeling plaster and crumbling stucco. Across the river, the spikes and green dome of the Parliament jabbed a low gray sky, a luminous red star like a Christmas tree ornament perched atop the cupola.

Anna turned away from the river, back toward the Buda

hills where she used to live. She passed a tawny-colored
neoclassical villa badly in need of paint and divided into
apartments. A woman in a bright print housecoat appeared
in a window. Her face was broad and seemed chiseled from
a different material than a Western face, than Anna's face
had become. Above the woman's elbows, flesh jiggled as she
plucked dead leaves off her window box geraniums. Suddenly she noticed Anna and gave her a peculiar, probing
look. Does she know I am one of her people? Anna wondered.

Dusk rolled over the city and grimy neon signs of a
garish blue began to flicker on. They drooped from somber
gray buildings, meant only to house, not to offer beauty. All
were built on a comforting scale, Anna thought. Humanity
is dwarfed by neither architecture nor technology here. On
this first day back, even cars, snub-nosed Trabants and box-
like Ladas, struck her as harmless toy models.

You can do yourself damage, she thought, leading a life
too rich in experiences and places. She wondered if she was
still capable of strolling peacefully alongside any river for
long. A man in a cheap leather coat (State issue?) moved
slower, more deliberately than the rest. They locked eyes for
a breath. It did not trouble her too much, however, the
prospect of being followed. That, too, was part of her city
and part of her childhood. Part of the legacy she wanted to
claim. She began to climb the steep steps that lead from the
Danube up to the Fisherman's Bastion. From there, she
recalled, you had the clearest view of the river and the city
it slashes in two. Once she had taken those steps two by two.
Now she reached the top out of breath.

Anna breathed deeply. She faced a row of six- and seven-story buildings with gray slate roofs. Turn-of-the-century housing without elevators, into which people are born, live, and die. These were not stepping stones toward bigger, shinier places. They contained an entire universe. She envied the residents' well-defined boundaries, their total ignorance of upward mobility.

How could a place change not at all, when she had changed so much? By what right did *this* view still move her, when neither the Manhattan skyline nor the roofs of Paris did anymore?

Two weeks earlier, Anna had been the center of attention at a Long Island dinner party full of this season's celebrities: cynics in well-worn jeans or jumpsuits heavy with zippered pockets. They sang for their supper with scathing observations on the human condition, as defined by the salons of Park Avenue and the bleached sundecks of the Hamptons. Anna had been avid for their attention. Who, then, was this woman entranced by a bleak cityscape, peopled by men and women who might no longer recognize her as one of their own?

She loved this city with the sort of possessive bond she did not feel for any other place, despite the memory of the searchers and their careless knives. The image of her father made small by fear, confessing to a crime he was not guilty of, was indelible. He had whispered "Yes" to the charge of spying for the "Imperialists," when in fact all he had done was file stories for an American magazine with permanent circulation troubles.

Anna had never forgotten the two lonely years she spent as the ward of strangers while her parents were prisoners of the State. And still she loved this place.

"Budapest?" her father, a widower now, alone in a book-lined West Side New York apartment, had sounded shocked when she told him. "Anna, you have nothing to do with Budapest. New York is where you belong. Maybe Washington. Why Budapest?" They had stopped hearing each other. It hurt, for she admired and needed her father's iron certainties (which ranged from gardening to euthanasia, but meticulously sidestepped the murky areas of emotions). His ambiguous silences and restrained approval had been the goad in both her personal and her professional life.

For example, how much did his comment about Sam, known to him from various talk shows ("Now there is a fellow who seems to have it all. An incisive mind, a certain *elegance* about him, don't you think, Anna?"), how much did her father's rare praise have to do with Anna and Sam's subsequent meeting (maneuvered by Anna) and the marriage that followed exactly one year later? Anna had known so little about her father then. He was the man whose affection and approval she most needed. And neither was readily forthcoming.

She would have sounded pathetically romantic, explaining her motives to him. ("What? A quest for your *roots?*" he would have asked, slicing the word with contempt, giving it the sound of an infection.) How to explain her discomfort with a country he deemed to be his family's final salvation? There was no point in explaining. His own inability to share their common heritage was partly responsible for the emptiness she felt, the feeling that one part was missing. That, too, would sound soggy. Shamefully sentimental.

"I've got a pretty interesting assignment for UNS," she

told him instead. There, you see. I'm no ordinary refugee floating in a bath of nostalgia, eager to annoint my Magyar spirit in the Danube's waters. "The Hungarian Ministry of Information," she told her father with measured self-importance, "has already accredited me as correspondent." His face was so clean of any expression, so set in determined indifference, she recognized how deeply he opposed her going.

The curled, dry leaves of late autumn crumpled under her feet as she slowly circled the massive equestrian statue of St. Stephen, founder of the Kingdom of Hungary. The people who passed her looked with unabashed interest at each other and at Anna. She loved the faintly Eastern cut of their features, the exciting possibility that in a prior life they might have met. On none of these faces did she recognize that hangdog look she had observed in other corners of the Eastern Bloc, a look imitated perfectly by the passengers on Manhattan subways.

Unlike Vienna, a city heavy with death and decay, Budapest seemed to bristle with life. These people, gallantly shabby, looked as if they deliberately defied a system as lifeless as the leaves they trampled. Anna smiled at a couple locked in passionate embrace in front of St. Matthew's Cathedral. She was filled with a vague sense of longing. For what? Not Sam, her estranged husband, whose last words to her had been, "Well, I never really believed you'd pull it off. This Hungarian number. Knock 'em dead, kiddo." Sarcasm had become the easy substitute for emotions between them. No, she felt only relief out of Sam's reach.

Were these then "her" people in their rough, cloth coats (how many times had hems and buttons been shifted to keep up with fashions seen in thumbed, greasy magazines from "out there"?) and their carefully polished boots? She felt as though she had lived a thousand lives since she left here. Lived like an impersonator who immerses herself in a role, gets it right, and then moves on. A sudden chill made her draw up the collar of her soft camel-hair coat so it nearly touched her nose.

Her hotel was just around the corner from the cathedral. Its chrome, glass, and Muzak imitation of a Hyatt House momentarily soothed her. It was bland and safe and familiar. She might have been in Atlanta. The bellboys looked at her with a mixture of familiarity and distance. Perhaps it was her eyes which told them she was one of them? "Those Tartar eyes," Sam had called them once, long ago, before the resentment of everything that made her different had set in, "they give you away. You could never pass for a Daughter of the American Revolution with those eyes." She was sure it wasn't her body that entranced the bellboys. Her body fell far short of the soft voluptuousness men in that part of the world still appreciate. Anna's long legs, slim hips, and breasts considerably reduced after a year of nursing Sarah, gave her a look that could be described as either undernourished or *elegant*. Her father's favorite adjective. She had begun to loathe it.

There was one message waiting for her, and she now returned the call. "Christopher Shepherd," he answered his own phone. His voice was well modulated, beyond surprise or enthusiasm. "Mrs. Winters suggested I ring." (The wife of the American Ambassador, Anna recalled.) As polite as he sounded, he managed to imply this was a duty call. "Do you like opera?" Anna loved opera, but this was not a man with whom she would share any loves. "It's *Rigoletto*," he added.

Because *Rigoletto* occupied a considerable place in Anna's memories of this city, and because she really didn't have anything else planned, she agreed to meet him that evening.

Four

ANNA WAS not sure what she had been expecting. He, at any rate, was not it. The United States Commercial Attaché did not look the part. He had none of the military blandness Anna associated with diplomats. Christopher Shepherd, deep in a leather chair, his long legs stretched out in front of him, was buried behind the back issue of a literary journal she could never get around to really reading. He rose slowly when she approached, appraising her with a steady, noncommittal look before he spoke. "Christopher Shepherd," he said impersonally, still not moving his eyes from hers. He had the slouch of a man who had reached his full height too early. His unself-conscious movements did not seem to belong to a bureaucrat.

With a neutral hand on her arm, Shepherd guided her out of the gleaming lobby. Anna automatically scanned the parking lot for a flash of State-issue leather, but saw none. She would have liked someone to take note of the embassy's interest in her.

Shepherd easily negotiated the hairpin turns of the drive from the top of the Castle district to the mouth of the tunnel, carved theatrically into the Buda Hill. He seemed comfortable with the silence between them. Not a man who strains for small talk, Anna thought. She guessed him to be in his late forties, though he might well have been a decade older. At any rate, he fell into that category of men no longer young but still youthful, a category still vastly more generous toward men than women. His hair was dark but heading toward the color of steel. His features were too even, and she assumed had once been of the standard handsome-man category she had never found appealing. The fine lines which etched his brow and cut his cheeks had long since rescued him from that mold. A certain fatigue around the eyes, a lack of shine in their blue center contradicted the still limber body.

"I used to hold my breath when we crossed the river," Anna said as they approached the Chain Bridge, with its outsized stone lions. "As a child, I was never sure when those lions would abandon their perch and chase our car."

"I had almost forgotten. You grew up here, didn't you? You seem more American than I am. Aren't all you TV reporters supposed to hail from the Heartland?"

"It's done with smoke and mirrors, for the sake of the cameras. My audience isn't supposed to know I'm a highly trained impersonator of an All-American Girl," she said, knowing there was more than a germ of truth in this.

"And the city?" Shepherd asked, "has it changed much since your childhood?" They had pulled up in front of the sprawling Baroque opera house, a twin of the Vienna State Opera.

"Everything seems much brighter than in my memories. People and buildings seem to have sprung out of Stalinist gloom. The big clean-up must have begun after the '56

Revolt," she mused. "Winners or losers, I guess nobody
wanted to be reminded of what happened here. There was
enough pain to go around." She could still conjure up the
sharp pain the sight of the long, implacable line of Soviet
tanks, rumbling off the Danube's bridges had caused her.
Budapest was theirs again. "Like a memory of a hopeless
love in your youth. When you grow up, you don't want any
mementoes around." Did he understand what she meant?
She searched his eyes for a life sign. He was absorbed in
parking his old BMW.

They walked up the circular stairs to the opera. In the
red-carpeted, gold-frosted foyer, almost inadvertently she
slipped her arm through his. "I . . . I spent so much time
here. Back then," she tried to explain. "As far as my parents
were concerned, the opera was far more vital to my develop-
ment than the playground." She had pressed his arm to
remind herself this was here and now. She was Anna Bator,
age thirty-six. A woman of the world. Citizen of the United
States. Network correspondent. He looked at her for the
first time with more than polite interest. By now, she was
somewhere else. Her eyes scanned the room, sniffed the air,
thick with the smell of powder and dust, the universal scent
of the theater. Perspiring men rested hands on soft hips and
fleshy arms. Behind a wreath of smoke, she made out a blur
of faces peering at her, just like the last time she was here.
Shepherd moved her hand from his arm into his own dry
palm. "C'mon, let's find our seats."

Like cool water on Anna's charged emotions, the haunt-
ing strain of the Verdi overture washed away the smoke and
the clatter. She tried to locate the box where she had sat
when her Uncle Pali conducted *Rigoletto*. It was the week
of her mother's arrest. Opera was the only way her uncle

knew how to distract her. Straight as a pitchfork, she had sat in the conductor's box. Her uncle had placed her within viewing range of the thickset, bemedaled figures upon whom all eyes were fixed. Anna always knew what was expected of her. She wore the solemn visage appropriate to her new status as political orphan.

Afterwards, Uncle Pali took her backstage to introduce her to the cast. She had suddenly turned shy, wrapped herself in one of Pali's tails, turned in it as if it were a curtain. She felt so unprotected. She had never been without her mother and father. A wash of grotesquely powdered faces beamed down at her. Hands and arms were outstretched, wide bosoms closed in on her. "When will they come home?" Anna blubbered into Pali's black trousers. "I want to go home," she cried, knowing that without her parents, home did not exist. The strain of the week had burst through the dam of her well-behaved child's masquerade. She was so miserable in the care of strangers. She missed her parents painfully.

"How could they, Pali?" she asked. Uncertain whether she meant the State or her parents who had allowed this to happen to them, Pali stroked her curly head. "They'll be back. You'll see, Anna. You must be brave a little bit longer." But she did not want to be brave. She wanted to sit in her mother's silky lap. Sniff her perfume. Smell her father's English cigarettes.

"Come here, sweetheart!" the generously proportioned soprano who, as Rigoletto's daughter, Gilda, had been carried offstage in a sack moments before, now scooped her up. "Your parents are too smart and this place is too stupid for them to be gone for long!" The diva smacked her moist, pink lips against Anna's wet cheek. Turning to no one in particular, she said, "Really, taking parents away from their children! What sort of a place is this?"

A few days later, the soprano's cleaning lady reported her missing. In addition to her outspoken views on the regime, the diva had also spent too many evenings after the opera in the company of a British diplomat. "The worst part," her Uncle Pali had told Anna, "is that no one even mentions it. A lion could be loose backstage, it could start nibbling on the entire chorus, and these days people would just walk around it. Nobody wants to notice anything."

A light pressure on her shoulder stirred Anna from her reverie. "That dress of yours," Shepherd whispered, "was meant for an overheated Georgetown house," he was tucking her cape around her shoulders, "not the Hungarian State Opera."

Afterwards, they drove along the Lenin Boulevard. In Anna's childhood, it had been the Stalin Boulevard. Shepherd had suggested dinner at the freshly restored Café Hungaria (which Anna's father still called by its old name, the New York).

"You know," Anna said, in search of a neutral subject, "the only workers with real incentive here are the sign painters. They're always in demand. Often the first to know which way the political winds are blowing. This street, for example," she pointed toward a narrow, badly lit strip, "was once Pannonia Street. Then they rehabilitated Laszlo Rajk, the former Foreign Minister, who was hanged for allegedly being Tito's agent in Budapest." Shepherd's face remained set in mild interest; Anna pressed on. "The fastest and least expensive way to make up for that little error was to paint over a street sign and name it Rajk. The painters have never been idle since the beginning of the Revolution. Whitewash

Tito, blackout Stalin. Change Mao to Lenin. Khrushchev to Brezhnev. They've got their brushes poised to see how many Brezhnev Boulevards survive the Andropov, Chernenko, and Gorbachev periods."

She fell silent, tired of the effort to draw him out. They entered the Café Hungaria, a flamboyant marriage of Byzantine, Rococo, and Baroque, the fruit of the Magyar cultural explosion of the nineteenth century. Somehow it worked, she thought: the wild disarray of twisted marble columns, the gilded ceiling and waiters in shiny black suits, pirouetting among wobbly, marble-topped tables. Or it must have worked when the Hungaria had been thick with smoke and the buzz of real conversation, when the electricity of a heated argument made the precarious little tables vibrate on the slippery tiles. Béla Bartók, André Kertész, Arthur Koestler, and scores of other writers, journalists, and musicians had all practiced and preened on this stage, before seeking the more intense testing of Montparnasse or Greenwich Village. Anna thought the small handful of customers who sat now in a prim half-circle looked like so many obedient bit players on a film set.

"Somehow," Shepherd finally cut into the long quiet, "the place reminds me of an old lady with a nearly perfect facelift."

They did not speak much in the car on the way home either. Nor did he consult Anna when he turned up the steep Hill of Roses to his own house. She had to admit feeling relief at not having to return just yet to the antiseptic luxury of her room. She sensed its meticulous reproduction of an American hotel wouldn't prevent her, alone, at night, from feeling exposed.

Slowly, the silence between them began to weigh less

heavily upon her. Perhaps, she thought, for this man, silence is as acceptable as social banter is for others. She, who had been trained to keep words floating in the air like a juggler, felt, perhaps for the first time, relieved of that responsibility.

His living room offered a postcard view of the Danube. The city beneath them was nearly black. "They only light it up on Saturdays now," Shepherd said. "All the Socialist Sisters are paying the price of Poland's fiscal bungles."

He handed her a cognac and settled on the couch next to her. "It *is* beautiful," he said, looking out, "this place and its long, sad history." He shifted his weight on the couch so he faced Anna's profile. "And your history? Is it like that?"

She was startled by the question, which was free of irony. It really acknowledged her for the first time. She thought, he has no small talk, this man, he reserves speech for actual communication. It pleased her that he would compare her in some way to this incomparably beautiful city and its rich and textured history. She smiled. For there was something peculiar about him, a piece which did not fit with the rest and which intrigued her. At that moment, she decided she would like him to fall in love with her. "Neither all that long, nor particularly sad," she said, not yet prepared to go deeper. "Like most."

Nor did she want to think about the ice-cold, sleepless nights with Sam. Always at night, when there was no escape or diversion. "Sh, darling, please, you'll wake Sarah," Anna always pleaded. But there was often some terrible betrayal that he accused her of. Dinner-party betrayals, which were the springboard for his profound dissatisfaction with her. "Anna, you stayed in the dining room, the two of you," he would start, "when the rest of us moved out. What were you talking about?" She was tempted to reply, "We rolled under the table in full view of the four Filipino caterers." But she knew there was no point. Not at night when he was stripped of humor, affection, and humanity. At night he was wrapped only in anger and a sense of having been cheated by the world, his early and diamond bright promise unfulfilled. Just as she, Anna, was finally on the short list of those who no longer had to loot, pillage, and rape for air time. What Sam did not understand was how little joy she had lately had in her success.

Her meaningless infidelities were not the source of this burning late night resentment. For she had become adept at secrecy. They were a small airhole in her suffocating confinement. An hour's escape with a trusted friend miraculously able to stir her into passion and forgetfulness. Whose existence in her life, she knew, was assured only by Sam's corrosive presence. Nothing more. Occasionally, she admitted to herself she didn't much like what she was becoming, either.

To the world, they were still a beautiful couple. The thoroughbred Philadelphia lawyer (who would surely make partner next time around) and the radiant reporter with an obscure but faintly dramatic past. How she had loved him. Loved his blond, square-shouldered, effortless perfection. His rocklike security. (Security was important to a woman with memories of a refugee child who hoarded plastic knives and forks on the airlift from Munich to Camp Kilmer, New Jersey. She was not yet privy to the rules governing the throwaway culture in those days.) What a challenge it had been to stir hidden depths in Samuel Caldwell III: a remarkable piece of American sculpture. His rogue's grin had once warmed every bone in her body.

There had been one unmistakable moment, its truth incandescent. It was then she had decided to return to Budapest on her own or not at all.

They had been dining at her in-laws' home in Villanova. The Caldwells lived in a Tudor mansion better suited as a backdrop for a sit-com about the travails of the squirearchy than real life. Everything was in its place, reflecting a high gloss, particularly the lady of the house, Loulie Caldwell. They were parents with no truths to pass on to their young, nor even much interest in them. Anna's father-in-law affected slurred Etonian speech and dropped his voice to a whisper for weighty pronouncements. He had come to Philadelphia many years earlier from across the Delaware River. Years of playing polo for Penn, marriage into one of the oldest families on the Main Line, and the helm of a pedigreed bank had not erased from his memory more humble beginnings in Camden, New Jersey. He did not appreciate Anna's irreverence toward the sanctity of Old Philadelphia.

Over bland jellied consommé (all effort went into the perfection of the table setting, "the presentation," and none into the food) they had been discussing the new district attorney. The D.A. was cut from the same cloth as Sam. St. Mark's, Princeton, the Merion Cricket Club, summers at Bar Harbor. Only Richardson Osborne's hands were never in his pockets. Brash and ambitious, he was impatient with the dinosaur-like pace of life in the Delaware Valley. He had subpoenaed three corporate presidents and two members of the elder Caldwell's club during his first week in office. He was also Anna's lover. That particular detail almost escaped her recollection of the evening.

"He's making a big mistake," Eliot Caldwell whispered to the reverently hushed dining room. "Osborne has to slow down or he'll lose the city's support."

As usual, no one around the polished mahogany table raised a voice in dissent. The Old Man was obviously not finished. Anna's husband and her mother-in-law probed deeper into their consommés.

Anna's thoughts drifted to a different family and a different dining room. It was a much smaller room, with far too much furniture. Unmatched pieces lovingly collected by generations, unhindered by decorators. Some of it was Baroque; some of it, the massive sideboard, Dutch; some, Biedermaier. Too many paintings. Everything in that room spoke of another time, a more gracious lifestyle. But the food on the table smelled like real food. Oh, the rich perfume of cream and paprika! And the conversation was real, too. None around that old table spoke in the solemn, priestly tones of a Philadelphia banker. Mother and father and daughter all had equal share in the storytelling, the laughter, and the interruptions. "Anna, we are not just talking about Galsworthy." The father leaned toward his child, excited. It was important that she understand. "We are talking about a way of life! Someday we will take you there. To London and, who knows, maybe even New York!" The child basked in self-importance. Her father spoke to her as an equal, and with an animation that had long since drained out of his voice.

"I think he's on the right track," Anna returned to her father-in-law in a tone of calm provocation. "If he drops it now, Philadelphia will just stay a second-rate railway station between New York and Washington. And Richardson Osborne will accept a job offer from the Justice Department."

Eliot Caldwell displayed his most benevolent, patriar-
chal smile. His complexion, however, nearly matched the
deep scarlet of his linen trousers. "You really understand,"
he said softly, "very little about Philadelphia." That was the
Old Man's ultimate statement of contempt. Anna looked
across the sparkling table at her silent husband and thought:
Maybe I don't want to understand Philadelphia. Or you or
your father or your mother. Maybe I am here by mistake.
And maybe it's not too late?

The only sound in the candlelit temple of the dining
room was made by Sally, the vigorous black lady who had
been with the family since Sam's birth. She rattled the Spode
soup bowls all the way to the kitchen. Anna looked at Sam
and wondered, What on earth did I have in mind, when I
married this stranger?

"Would you like another?" Shepherd poured them both
more cognac. "Here's to you, Anna Bator," he said, touching his snifter to hers, his voice cognac warm. "I have a
feeling you may just live up to your name."

"Your Hungarian is advanced enough to know," Anna
said, smiling with childish pleasure, "that Bator means
brave?"

"Yes," he said, fingertips brushing her cheek.

He drove her back to the hotel. There were no bellboys
blocking the entrance and even the doorman had signed off.
She leaned over to kiss him lightly on the cheek. He shifted
his face and his lips stayed on hers for a moment. She
jumped abruptly out of his car, as if she had just touched a
scalding surface. "I'll ring you in the morning," he called
after her. She was already gone.

Five

SHE LAY ON the crisp yellow Hilton sheets, her eyes fixed on the ceiling in dry wakefulness. Her mind was a projection room of conversations, moments screened, rewound and played back again, obsessively reviewing scraps from the past, recent and long gone. Returning to Budapest had been the obvious solution to a problem she still had trouble defining. For a long time, Budapest had not been of much interest to her at all.

Giving up on sleep, Anna got out of bed and parted the Hilton's thick linen curtain. Looking out toward the river crawling beneath the Buda hill she recalled the odd starting place for the journey back.

She had started crying in Bridgehampton. She had been flipping through a pile of records at Caldor's. From a speaker a black voice sang "That's No Way to Say Good-bye" and bathed the airless, neon and vinyl arcade in its honeyed warmth. Just a song. Banal and accessible. Not for all time. Yet the song and its words about endlessly scrapped dreams was enough to make her cry.

She continued crying during her solitary drive home on the traffic-clogged Long Island Expressway. Later that day, she stood in her East Side living room and still hoped Sam would perform a conjurer's trick, wrap her in an all-encompassing look of generous acceptance and make the rest recede like last night's dream. Finally accept all the layers, the ambitions, the strengths, and the still ill-defined yearning. Oh, he had no trouble with the weaknesses. He could be so consoling when she was on the brink of rejection. "You're the best, sweetheart," he would whisper into the telephone, his office the scene of an international conference call, "those bastards don't know what they have," when her interview with a renegade guerrilla chief did not make the air. "If they don't treat you right, somebody else will. Come home. I love you." And she would fly home, feeling all was right in the world.

But now his eyes narrowed and he tossed back his head the way he did when he imagined betrayal. "How was your weekend?" he asked, but didn't wait for her answer. "We managed just fine, Sarah and I. Without you." His hurt was too transparently wrapped in arrogance.

"Levin rang last night. I've got the Budapest assignment," she said without emotion. "UNS came through."

She felt like a cheat saying this; incapable of a healing gesture, yet afraid to cut clean. But with Sam she always sought the easy way out. She did not think he could absorb what was really on her mind. Or, to be more honest, she wasn't brave enough to try to tell him.

"Shall I come?" he asked, his voice unusually tentative.

"What did you say?"

"Shall I come with you? To Budapest. Do you want me along?"

Oh no, she wanted to say. No. You have nothing to do with this trip.

"That's really nice of you, Sam," she said. "Right in the middle of two mergers. I'm touched by the offer. Really." Why was he confusing her now that she was finally pulling together the courage to break with him?

"There's bound to be a lot of emotional stuff involved in this trip," he said, running his fingers through his light brown hair. "Might be nice to have a friendly face along. What do you say, sweetie?"

"Yes," she said, "there will be some emotional stuff."

She looked across a narrow alley into a dimly lit scene in the next building. A man and a woman sat in armchairs facing each other. There was nothing distinguished about either of them; an ordinary couple in a drab decor. A tall floor lamp cast a harsh light on their faces. They were reading. Every so often they looked up at each other. Anna could tell they were in love from the way they held their eyes on each other and from the frequency with which they looked up. They made it look easy. Two plain people in an austere room who seemed to fit both with each other and their setting.

"I don't think it's a good idea, Sam," she said at last. "I haven't been very straight with you for a while. What has happened between us is as much my fault as yours. But I'm tired of . . . of . . . a lot of things," she said without looking at him.

"The work it takes to keep us going," she added. It made

her feel strangely lightheaded, to be so bold. The thought of her trip gave her courage.

"I thought you were pretty happy with things," he said, "I mean, we're both so busy . . . maybe we should take more time out. . . ."

"Well, yes, maybe we should. But it's really something else. It's just that I really haven't been *right* for some time. I don't know how to explain this . . . things seem to move me in strange ways these days. Bits of music. A word with associations . . . I feel something happening inside . . . And I don't know where it's coming from. . . ."

He looked at her without any malice or comprehension, his brows furrowed in concern. He would have given her the same look had she announced she had a malignant tumor.

"It's not your fault, Sam," she repeated. "But I'm not exactly what you think I am. What *I* thought I was. Oh, I know I have the job everybody wants. The husband women envy. All this . . ." she said, her arm sweeping in the airy, perfectly understated living room, suitable for any young couple with unlimited prospects. "It's not working for me. I want to be someplace where I don't have to push all the time just to be dealt in the game. Where people have a memory. And a history . . ." Her voice was about to break, so she turned away and looked again out the window at the couple across the alley. She envied them the way they seemed to fit together and into that room. The way she had envied Zsuzsi's family as a child, the assurance with which they occupied their places.

"We don't even laugh at the same things, Sam. No,

seriously. Humor is a very serious thing. What's more serious? Maybe air and water. . . ."

She knew he wasn't following any of this. They didn't have the habit of talking about things that mattered. Just then, Sam looked so mystified, stripped of his habitual complacency. She remembered what she had loved about him: this absolute innocence.

"I fooled us both," she said to his back, which looked like a wall. "I'm somebody different. I feel it." She paused but still he said nothing. "No, I don't think it's a good idea, your coming with me to Budapest."

The two armchairs in the room across the alley were empty now. The floor lamp still cast a hard circle of brightness on them. Anna imagined the couple already locked in fierce but tender love. "Knock 'em dead, kiddo," she heard Sam shout from the front door. He had recovered. She heard the door close behind him. Anna walked down the hall and, careful not to wake her, lay down next to Sarah.

Six

ANNA SPREAD HER HANDS ON the cold windowpane and stared blindly at the red star atop the Parliament's dome. The only light in the Budapest night sky.

The trouble was her assimilation was nearly seamless. She had none of the immigrant's hard vowels or rough edges. With her parents' encouragement, she had applied herself so diligently to the task that not a cultural hair was out of place in her transformation. She glowed with the ease of those born into place and position. And this was precisely the problem. She had begun to chafe under this smooth finish. She felt there was something buried under it which she had never touched, which neither her friends nor her husband ever asked her about. Nor had she volunteered any of it.

Eastern Europe was not a burning topic in the New York of the eighties. Had Anna been Nicaraguan or Cambodian or even Afghan, they would have shown more interest in the trauma of her experience. But the human tide that had washed her here had receded many years ago. She was supposed to have made her peace by now. The trouble was she *hadn't.* Because, until now, the whole business was less compelling for Anna Bator than any of those other, more fashionable catastrophes. An interest in them would get her not only air time, but acceptance into those places where she used to feel she belonged.

She engineered the Budapest assignment with an ease that came from years of maneuvering and manipulating to get her way. Throughout her professional life she had used all tools available: humor, compassion, an implied, never-quite-delivered sexuality, and ultimately, the assurance that she'd come through with an extra inch of insight and intelligence.

"There's a lot of sex appeal," she had told Abe Levin, her executive producer at UNS, "in the old home-town girl makes good story. Especially when the home town is still a Soviet barracks." She could tell from the warm twinkle in his eyes the proposal was well timed. He was either finally having his way with the ambitious production assistant who had resisted his charms longer than most, or the Redskins had trounced Miami the night before. She could see him mentally composing the press release: "Anna Bator, former Hungarian refugee, returns to Budapest. Exclusive, five-part UNS Up-Close report, starts tonight."

"Take your crew to the Vaci Street," he said, leaning so far back in his chair he was nearly horizontal. Anna knew she had the assignment. "And just have them shoot all those braless girls in T-shirts for me." He smiled his most benevolently lascivious smile. "I was there in 1968, looking for reaction to the Czech thing. That's what I remember. Hungarian tits and ass."

"If they've got them, we'll get 'em, Abe," she said

matching his leer with her brightest smile. "I also have another thought, in a slightly different vein. Every nook and cranny of the Holocaust has been covered and docudramaed to death, except the Hungarian chapter, which in some ways was the most brutal . . . in terms of speed and surprise. If I can find a couple of eyewitnesses and enough human stuff, will you give me some air time?"

"Yeah, well let's first see what you come up with," Levin answered, one eye already scanning a memo in front of him. "Just stay in close touch and don't trust their phones, huh?"

"This is my old territory remember," Anna answered coolly. "For once you're sending the right person to the right place."

"Okay, big shot, leave the herograms to me. Safe trip," he said and reached for his phone.

Anna had been endowed with neither of Abe Levin's favorite attributes when she was left alone, the child of Enemies of the People. A pensioned couple, paid by the State to look after the children of political prisoners, her new "family." A tired, well-meaning pair, far more concerned about their own daughter (recently deported to a remote village for "ideological self-improvement") than about Anna. A little girl with oversized hazel eyes in a shiny black pinafore, eager to please to atone for her parents' shortcomings.

She sat in class, anxious and too well prepared. Comrade Barna, her white coat starched stiff as cardboard, continually brushed past her, ignoring Anna's rigid, raised arm. "Comrade Barna," Anna had whispered one morning, when the sharp edge of the teacher's white sleeve jabbed her cheek, "those are very pretty shoes." Since the State Store offered only two varieties of sturdy brown lace-ups to the people, she was sure her compliment would soften the teacher's resistance.

"Anna," Comrade Barna shot back, loud enough for the rest of the class to appreciate the reproof, "if you spent more time on fractions and less admiring my shoes," the teacher was already at the blackboard, not even looking in the little girl's direction, "it's possible we might get along better."

She was not going to give the teacher the satisfaction of seeing her cry. Anna dug her nails deeper into her palm. But now she knew for certain she had been condemned along with her parents as anti-State. Anti-People. Some sort of a mastodon resisting the inevitable. So, really, there was no further point in saving face anymore. She allowed herself the thin reward of unchecked tears. But Comrade Barna's large, capable hand, in firm command of chalk, was already scraping arcs on the blackboard, her back to the child.

She never said goodbye to her Uncle Pali. It was too late now. Pali had died of cancer two years before Anna's return. She recalled their last time together. Anna and her parents (unexpectedly, ecstatically freed two weeks earlier) had spent that night in the American diplomatic residence next door to their apartment house. Don Apple was to drive them across the Austro-Hungarian frontier the next morning. Anna's father had mysteriously acquired passports for all three of them. "They've finally realized we're more trouble to them here than abroad," he had explained. "Good riddance, they told me."

Anna was flushed with the night-before-Christmas excitement of an imminent adventure. She was getting her first

English lesson from the Apple children. "Hello!" she chanted proudly. "My name is Anna!" Suddenly, Uncle Pali, shapeless and sad and out of place in that bright American home, was framed by the front door. He who was staying behind had come to say goodbye.

"Goodnight!" Anna shouted at him carelessly, bounding up the stairs. "Goodnight?" he asked, imitating her newly acquired English. "What do you mean, 'Goodnight'?" Anna knew exactly what she meant. She meant she did not wish to hug this potbellied, gray-haired uncle with his hangdog look in front of the Apple children in their Davy Crockett pajamas with the feet stitched on. What would these tow-headed, carefree children think if they saw her uncle, a grown man whose voice did not sound very steady, weep at the parting from his niece?

Though Uncle Pali's two-room apartment had made it impossible for Anna to move in with him, he had taken her to the opera, to *Rigoletto*, when others were afraid to be seen in her company. Now Pali had become an encumbrance. His gloomy visage reminded her that she was, after all, still a little Hungarian girl. And Anna was ready for America! She could not grasp what Pali knew: That they would never see each other again.

Tears streamed from her sleepless eyes. Good Lord, she thought, some crazy broad I turned out to be. Tears for the crumbling immigrant's dream? Or for the absence of anything with which to replace it? Oh, she knew why she had come. She had come for that which everyone but she seemed to possess. Others seemed made of more solid stuff than she who seemed to exist only by their consent. She straddled cultures and countries so adroitly, yet never claimed her own. The Little Princess of her Socialist childhood had been deftly transformed into the All-American Girl. And always, in the back of her mind, this thought: What if they find out I am something else?

Shortly before daybreak, she finally drifted off to sleep. She awoke, looked around the anonymous room, and felt immense relief. It was a far safer place than where her dream had taken her. In her dream she had fallen asleep in the back seat of her car. The gathering thunder of a galloping horse, stronger and more menacing as it approached, aroused her. She looked up to see a deserted landscape of rolling hills broken only by a clump of dark trees outlined in black against a low sky. Then, the trunk of a horse, as dark as the sky, its muscular curves expanding as it closed in on her car. She could not see the horse's rider. Frozen in fear, her head on the seat, she waited for the horse and its still invisible rider to pass. The horse, however, planted itself alongside her car and blacked out her vision. The rider's booted leg pressed against her door. All she could see were the olive drab pants of a uniform. Her heart was pumping so wildly she was certain he would hear it.

Seven

EDITH FEKETE was the kind of bureaucrat any state machine sifts rapidly from the rest into a position of high responsibility. She was unflappable, bloodless, and impatient with original thought. For this first meeting she had already committed Anna Bator's background to her mental computer. Her aggressively monotone greeting let Anna know she knew.

"Sit down, please," Comrade Fekete, in a tone both unctuous and mildly threatening, motioned her toward a fifties-style imitation Danish modern armchair. Everything about her spoke of her contempt for détente, peaceful coexistence, or socialism with a human face. Her face was assertively plain, her lips nearly invisible beneath a wispy curtain of soft brown. Her hair was styled in the tight curls not often seen since Stalin and home permanents simultaneously fell out of favor. Her hands resting primly on her laminated wood desk, she waited for Anna to begin.

"Without a permanently accredited crew," Anna said, trying to avoid the hypnotic gaze of the omnipresent Lenin peering over Comrade Fekete's shoulder (Anna wondered if Stalin was on the flip side, waiting to turn over), "I'm pretty much useless here." It was a relief for her to be sitting in a sterile office, as stark as an art gallery stripped of pictures, carrying out the sort of mindless task that was part of her job and required no imagination. For a split second she shut her eyes, which felt dry and hot. The long night had left her limp, blurring lines between reality, imagination, and memory.

As head of Hungarian Radio and Television's International Division, Edith Fekete had the power to determine the size of each of the dozen or so foreign news agencies in Budapest. They both knew the reason Anna Bator had been granted permission to set up shop in the capital. The State Department had recently accredited a Hungarian journalist in the United States. He was less known for his by-line than for his impeccable Party connection.

"You know," Comrade Fekete spoke with the infinite patience of a teacher dealing with a backward child, "you can choose from any number of our crews on a freelance basis. You have surely heard of our excellent film makers?" She flashed a smile that was almost enough to make Anna weep.

"I really think it is vital for me to have my own team," Anna held her ground, "so that we can move quickly when a story breaks." She would not accept one of Edith Fekete's in-house plants without a token protest at least.

"Oh, Miss Bator," Comrade Fekete's smile did not soften the implied menace in her voice. "You would be surprised how fleet-footed our boys can be!" I bet, Anna thought. When they're on your payroll.

"Well, there is also another . . . a technical . . . problem,"
Anna said in the staccato tone she normally reserved for
too-smooth politicians. "You see we don't shoot film anymore. We switched to videotape a few years back. Which
of course means our cameras are different from yours. In fact
the whole system, processing, editing, broadcasting, has
been transformed. In the States we can now go live from
anyplace. All we do is throw up the satellite dish that's
attached to one of our news vans. . . ." She noted with
satisfaction the darkening of Comrade Fekete's features at
the implied superiority of Anna's video revolution. "News
has become a twenty-four-hour operation. When something
breaks . . . boom, we're on. It's made my job a lot tougher,"
Anna went on, savoring her little commercial. "I haven't got
the time I used to while the film was in the 'soup' to think
about my piece and then write it. Now I start moving my
lips and just hope to God my mind follows pretty soon
after." She smiled brightly. "But you see your film crews,
however skilled I know them to be, are of no use to us under
the present system."

"Of course, we know all about these innovations,"
Fekete said, scowling. "But let us proceed one step at a time,
please. I would like you first to get a better understanding
of our country . . . quite different from the one you left as
a child, no? Before we start bringing in the vans and satellite
dishes."

"Just a crew. Two people, one to tape, one to do
sound. We just want to do some features. Nothing dramatic. We'll 'bird,' I mean satellite, out of Vienna when the
time comes. . . ."

Comrade Fekete made a sound with her lips like that of

a purse closing. The interview was over.

Anna breathed a deep sigh of relief. For her mind was beginning to stray from this confrontation. Her stomach was queasy with fatigue. Where was Christopher Shepherd this morning? That kiss seemed to come from nowhere. It was self-contained and without either expectation or promise. Did it make a lie of Shepherd's detachment? She could not think clearly. She touched her mouth involuntarily. She knew nothing about the man.

"Miss Bator," the ooze of Comrade Fekete's voice (she must be the last one left in Budapest who insisted on that anachronistic title) brought her back to the neon glare in the office of Hungarian Television. "We are not ruling out the possibility of the future expansion of your operations." Observing her, Anna understood more clearly than she ever had as a child why her parents could not support this cause. How could they rally behind a barricade manned by an army of such comrades? What did they have in common with such Spartan sanctimony, her brave and puzzling parents?

But they actually signed on with the "enemy" in the frostiest days of the Cold War. They had paid dearly for it, of course. And she along with them. Only the easing up that preceded the outbreak of the Revolution cut short their long prison sentences.

"I look forward to hearing from you soon," Anna said, rising. "And while I await permission to bring in a crew, I shall use my time to research the Holocaust story I outlined to you in my letter," she added in a tone as crisp as Comrade Fekete's own.

Eight

S̲HE WALKED OUT OF the great crumbling former
Stock Exchange building that houses Hungarian Radio and
Television, eager to put distance between herself and both
Comrades Fekete and Lenin. She crossed the green strip that
divides the two sides of Freedom Square. The reassuringly
familiar Stars and Stripes flapped in front of the graceful
cream-colored building facing the little park. She leaned
against the heavy gate with its intricate iron scrollwork and
faced a crew-cut Marine. He looked as solidly fixed as the
embassy itself. "Mr. Shepherd, please."

In minutes he stood in front of her with a smile that
made fine lines fan out from the corners of his eyes. He
looked as though he had been expecting her.

"Are you up to making a sentimental journey with me?"
They stepped into the bracing December sunlight. Then
they were back in his car, driving from Pest to Buda, up the
steep hill that led to Csaba Street.

"It may not look like much," she said, facing the five-
story stucco building, a monument to Socialist Realist bleak-

ness, "but this is where our favorite newsperson spent her first ten years."

At first sight it was just another drab building of a faded dun color. The inhumanity of her old home did not make it ideal for a rush of Proustian remembrances. She stood there blinking back the disordered emotions, waiting for a clearer impression of the old place. She recalled hanging upside down from the thick branch of that apricot tree. The tree, as well as the meager garden behind the high iron fence, seemed untouched by twenty-five years.

She suddenly fixed on one image, at first blurred, then in sharp focus. Age six or eight, she was perched high up in that apricot tree. Beneath her stood Joska, Zsuzsi's six-year-old brother. His head was freshly shaved to reveal surgical scars. "Jew!" a small band of her playmates taunted the little boy. Joska continued to hold his head to one side, in his look of permanent mystification. It was the first time she had heard the word "Jew." She assumed it meant creep.

Something else, a shard from the more recent past, pierced through her consciousness. On a sunny Saturday, not long before, she had been strolling through the dilapidated chaos of London's Portobello Market. On a table jumbled with dusty bric-à-brac, an object, exotic but inexplicably familiar, caught her eye. "What is that?" she asked the wine-flushed vendor in his tweed hacking jacket. She jabbed a finger toward the tarnished minaret-shaped artifact, no taller than a candlestick. "Oh, it's from the East," he answered with a bored shrug. "Used for spice burning, I'm told. Central European. Jewish." She had seen its double, that she knew. Only she could not then remember where. Now, in the bizarre course of memory's travels, she remembered an identical one that had stood on the sideboard of her old dining room, in the building she now faced.

She turned suddenly to look at Christopher Shepherd. He seemed in no hurry, nor in need of explanation. Not that she was in the mood to provide any. She was glad enough he was there. Anna motioned for him to follow up the stairs leading to the house, past the gate and around to the back. There she found what she had sought. The tall cyclone fence was topped by barbed wire several layers deep. "The house next door must still be an American diplomatic residence," she told him. Shepherd looked puzzled as she dropped to her knees and felt her way along the thickly ivy-covered fence. "There!" she exclaimed with a smile of victory. "It's still there. Here. You feel," she moved his hand to the spot. His arm disappeared through the thicket. "My God," he whispered, "that's a hole big enough for a man to squeeze through."

"As well as his wife and child," she told him. "That hole was supposed to have been our ticket to freedom," she said, rising from the ground. "Only it didn't work out that way."

Thirty years earlier, midnight arrests were a part of daily life in Budapest. A young American diplomat who routinely became more involved in the lives of locals than was good for his career had taken wire cutters to that fence. "When your turn comes, Alex," Donald Apple had told Anna's father, "you'll know the knock. Don't answer the door," Apple had warned. "Just grab Julia and Anna and make for the fence. We'll be ready on the other side." The fence never had a chance to play its heroic part. Alex Bator was kidnapped on the street corner where Shepherd's BMW was now parked.

They sat down on the peeling wooden bench which looked no more weathered than it had thirty years before. The bench still stood under the window from where Anna had witnessed her father's abduction.

Nine

THEY HAD BEEN GUESTS OF the American Ambassador that evening. Later, Anna's mother told her there had been subtle clues all evening that something was afoot. But by then, her parents were fairly convinced of their immunity to danger. They had developed the arrogance of survivors.

Lajos, the butler at the American Ambassador's Residence, opened the door to them with the exaggerated courtliness he reserved for the Bators. There was no mockery intended in the butler's excessive bowing and scraping. Quite the reverse. As a Hungarian he knew the risk the Bators ran, appearing at the Americans' doorstep so regularly. Courtliness above and beyond his custom was Lajos's way of showing them that he admired their courage.

Once again this Thursday, the two of them would be the only Hungarians to grace Phelps Lewis's salon. Alex and Julia Bator made up the Ambassador and Mrs. Lewis's weekly foursome for bridge. And Lajos was never certain he would see the Bators again, from Thursday to Thursday.

"Is everything all right, Lajos?" Alex Bator asked the silver-haired butler, as he led them up the mahogany-paneled staircase to the drawing room. The opulent residence had been built for a nineteenth-century composer, one of those rare artists whose work enabled him to construct a life of solid bourgeois comfort. For a while, during the last century, musicians were as integrated into the fabric of Budapest society as bankers and lawyers.

Succeeding American ambassadors and their ladies had systematically stripped away any reminders of the peculiarly Magyar blend of folklore and rococo. Now it looked like a suburban American vision of an English country house. The spacious sitting room with its soft beige sofas and chintz-covered armchairs would have been deemed acceptable by a Winnetka corporation lawyer's wife.

But it was not to this pale, nostalgic haven of Americana that the courtly butler led Bator. He pointed the way toward a small but immaculate powder room just off the salon. Lajos bent over the toilet, quickly flushed it, and simultaneously addressed Bator. "Doctor ur"—he used the title of respect of a world long since dead and buried to both the butler and the journalist—"they have asked me to file a report on this evening." He spoke rapidly, in the elliptical style of a man who knows his listener needs few explanations. "I had to agree or lose my job . . . you understand." Lajos shrugged his sagging shoulders. "This is all I know how to do."

Alex nodded. "Thank you, Lajos, and please don't worry. Julia and I really are looking forward to a good game of bridge." He patted the butler's back. "You'll just have to report our scores to the AVO. We intend to beat your employers, of course."

Lajos's was not the first confession of this sort Anna's father had heard. Their cook filed weekly reports on the couple's activities, with the Bators' help. Anna's father always said, it was the ones who did not let you know they were in the employ of the AVO, they were the ones you had to worry about.

"Hello, Alex," Ambassador Lewis drew him toward a welcoming fire at the far end of the room. "I was just beginning to work up the courage to tell your wife how amazingly beautiful she is. It sounded very much as though our dear Lajos had disposed of you in a most inelegant fashion. How are you, dear boy?" Lewis, his nose a crushed network of exposed capillaries, beaming goodwill, dropped the glad hand he had perfected years before on the New Haven campus across Bator's back.

"Thank you, Mr. Ambassador," he replied with a formal bow. Americans struck him as disturbingly hale. He invariably stiffened under this sort of bonhomie.

Julia Bator and Ethel Lewis were already sipping Scotches in their wing chairs. Julia's simple gray silk shirt and long black skirt with its deep slit made her look as sleek as a colt. It made no difference how mean the times were nor how scarce such mainstays of feminine splendor as stockings and cosmetics, Julia always managed to look luminous in an effortless sort of way. It was the green eyes, flecked with gold, which never stopped mocking either herself or the world around her, set off by high Magyar cheekbones and a mobile mouth that looked equally ready for full-throated laughter or warm kisses. Anna remembered her mother as a burst of life on the murky set that was Budapest in the fifties. (Later, only when she recollected details of her life in prison would Julia momentarily glow again. The memory of the horror and how she had held up under it would light up Julia's face and animate her voice in the old way.)

Ethel Lewis provided a flattering contrast to the Hungarian woman. Lacking for nothing in embellishments, the Ambassador's lady was a proponent of the more-is-more school of beauty. Her round, soft features were powdered and rouged into something resembling a well-frosted birthday cake. Her aqua print from Garfinkle's Designer Room would have looked more at ease covering a bay window than a female form.

The Bators decorated the American drawing room with such polish and ease they nearly succeeded in making the Ambassador forget who they were. Alex's shirts still came from Jermyn Street, compliments of a colleague at the *Daily Telegraph*. He no longer used the English tailor who had kept him in pinstripes before the war. Only the most discerning sartorial specialist could tell that his dark blue suit was of Budapest's Vaci Street manufacture.

"Why don't we go for a little stroll, Alex?" the Ambassador's arm was back around Bator's shoulder. "It'll clear my head for that trouncing I'm about to take from you and Julia." The Lewises were, by their own admission, no match for Anna's parents' superbly honed, imaginative bridge. The Ambassador obviously had something other than a bracing walk in mind.

The two men stepped onto the wide terrace which, in summer, was a furious blaze of Ethel Lewis's geraniums in every imaginable color. Lewis led the way down the steps across the cold, sodden grass to the overgrown tennis courts. Alex hoped that whatever the Ambassador had on his mind would not take long. Americans, he frequently grumbled, have the irritating habit of not believing in overcoats. The night chill cut right through his suit and stabbed his chest.

"I'd watch my step, dear fellow." Lewis spoke in a barely audible voice. "We can't put our fingers on anything firm, but the Company boys are sniffing something unpleasant at this end. You and Julia are custom-made targets for trouble. If they need to stir things up again."

"Thank you, Phelps. You are typically thoughtful and I won't take your words lightly. Only this is not the right time for your scenario. If they had wanted to use Julia and me as some sort of object lesson, they would have already done so. Remember, Stalin has been dead for two years now. If they have left us alone this long, why move now?" Alex rubbed his frozen hands together and tried to coax the Ambassador back toward the warmth of the apricot-and-beige drawing room.

"You're a brave pair, Alex," Lewis looked at him with emotion. "I do respect what you and Julia are doing. Those pieces about what it's really like behind the Curtain . . . There's nobody who would have kept at it as long as you have, without cracking. Oh, yes. I know you haven't got many Hungarian friends left. It's no secret you're a couple of pariahs in your own country." Lewis was finally leading him back into the house. "It can't be an easy life."

"No, but look at the rewards." Alex, ill at ease with emotions, forced a smile. "Bridge with you and Ethel once a week. A steady supply of Gillette blades and Pall Malls. It's not all sacrifice for the world's right to know what goes on in this God-forsaken country of ours." Anna's father knew his answer was not altogether facetious. He and Julia could not bear the thought of living the graceless lives of their fellow countrymen. As for the Ambassador's warning, surely no more than the usual misreading of routine Kremlin-floated rumors.

The Bators played an even more spirited game of bridge than usual that night. Their technique at the card table made the Americans' seem sluggish and clumsy. It was an expression of their love for each other, their virtuoso bridge game. You are a clever woman, Alex's eyes told his wife. And she, warmed by his pride in her, pushed herself to greater concentration and more breathtaking scores.

"Budapest, the Bators, and bridge," Phelps Lewis walked them down the staircase to the black-and-white-tiled foyer. "I shall always think of the three together. See you next Thursday." Lewis kissed Julia on both cheeks, a legacy of his previous posting in Paris.

Warm in her prewar sable, the afterglow of Scotch, and a well-played hand, she snuggled against her husband in the front seat of their Chevrolet (bought from an American diplomat recently declared persona non grata). After ten years of marriage and one child, she was still not immune to her husband's striking good looks. For all her apparent worldliness, she was a superstitious woman, who did not like to look at him for too long. He might vanish if she became too dependent on that melancholy charm of his. It was not a relationship in repose. Neither took the other for granted. They had already been through too much together. They understood that each day shared was an unexpected gift, which might easily be revoked. Alex squeezed her shoulder. Neither wished to break the moment's spell by speaking.

It had started snowing. Soon large, fluffy flakes blurred the scars that disfigured the city. The Bators' was the only car on the road. They loved this feeling of isolation from the day's net of commitments and masters.

The Chevrolet began its tentative climb up the steep, white-blanketed Buda Hill. Alex pulled into the driveway of the French Ambassador's Residence. M. Poncet had generously allowed them the privilege, since their own apartment house had no driveway. Julia sat waiting for Alex to help her out of the car. Suddenly, she noticed that the driveway and the street beyond were alive with dark figures closing in on them.

"Alex!" Julia screamed, leaping from the car into the snow. But by then a faceless figure had a tight grip on her husband's left arm, another gloved hand reached for his right. He looked ashen. And suddenly very old. His jaw went slack. "Let go of my arm!" he hissed at them. "Do you think I'm going to run away?"

Ten

Anna just sat there on the hard wooden bench beneath her old window, seemingly oblivious to Shepherd's presence. "Did they let you say goodbye to him?" he interrupted her long silence.

"Oh, no," she answered. "But I saw him. A prisoner." She looked away from him.

Whether it was the crunch of snow under tires or just the commotion in the air, something had woken her up. She reached the window just in time to see her mother leap from the car into the snow. She caught the terrible image of her father frozen like a rabbit trapped in headlights. Anna knelt there on her bed, hypnotized, hoping she was still asleep. For she often had dreams of her parents being taken away, punished for their independent spirit. They had hinted that someday they may not be there. She never really believed them, of course.

She couldn't leave the window. Somehow she thought that if she left and there were no witnesses at all, something really terrible might happen to her parents. So she just kept watching, too shocked to cry or to call out or to move.

Her mother finally shook off her stupor and moved quickly toward her husband. She put a hand on each of his cheeks and said, "I love you, my darling." Anna could see him lean toward her in an armless embrace. His arms weren't his anymore. The child stayed there and watched the car, without its headlights, with the fresh snow muffling its already quiet engine, blend noiselessly into the night. There was an unreal beauty to the street. Anna had never seen it look that way. The jewel bright sheen of the snow reflected a fat, friendly moon above. She wondered if it would be the last time her father would see the moon.

"A few minutes later, I heard the key turn in the front door and ran barefoot to see my mother walk in, five men behind her. She looked very composed, always calmer in crisis than under the empty weight of daily life. The secret policemen wore the blue uniform of municipal policemen." Her mother went to rouse the brittle Frenchwoman, who, in her capacity as governess, had been the poison of Anna's early years. Anna marveled at the speed with which Madame managed to smudge two perfect circles of rouge on her pasty complexion. The only thing she had overlooked in her haste was the red hairnet that kept her gleaming, dyed black hair in place while she slept.

Madame accepted her position as State's witness (a role that required, in the words of the curly-haired spokesman of the so-called municipal policemen, "ascertaining the legality and propriety" of the search) with a solemn nod of her raven head. "Later, we learned how well suited Madame had been for this assignment. For some time, it turned out, she had been padding her governess's wages by moonlighting for the AVO. I must admit this news came as belated vindication for me. I'd long suspected that only a woman with a criminal bent would raise the venetian blinds right above my head with as much clatter as she did at six-thirty every morning."

Her mother dropped into her favorite armchair and automatically reached for one of her Pall Malls, left on the table in front of her. A bored-looking agent, who until then had been coiled quietly in a corner, now sprang to life. He whipped the cigarette out of her hand and thrust one of his own at her. No telling what sort of devious Western poison she might administer to herself! Not on his watch. With a disdainful hand, Julia waved his Hungarian cigarette away.

Then the agents plunged into their real job. As if obeying an invisible choreographer, their hands vanished into pockets from which they emerged with compact pocket knives. They flicked their blades into the soft cushions of the Bators' living-room armchairs and sofas. "Don't!" Anna yelled helplessly as a blade was sunk into her battered rocking horse. The straw with which the sad animal was stuffed soon littered her room.

Then came the books. The searchers removed hundreds of them from shelves and painstakingly examined them for hidden notes between the pages, before they tossed them in a heap on the floor. The entire procedure came to a standstill when one of the agents emerged form the toilet brandishing Grace Kelly's radiant face on the cover of *LIFE*. Each of the agents felt obliged to search this issue himself, turned the pages showing the luminous princess with agonizing slowness. "D'you really think she's that good-looking?" one of them asked with a sneer.

In the kitchen, they emptied sugar and flour containers and unscrewed light bulbs. Her mother, dry-eyed but beginning to show signs of regretting her proud refusal of the AVO's cigarette, followed them each step of the way.

When they had finished, they bundled every letter, bill, and news report in the Bators' files, along with Alex's new Nikon, into suitcases they found in the apartment. The place looked as though it had been ravaged by an earthquake. It was no longer a home.

It must have been about seven in the morning when Julia said, "Get dressed, Anna. We have things to do." Her voice was flat. "She knew that she did not have much time before they would come back for her. I didn't go to school that day or for the rest of the week. My mother wanted me by her side. She knew they would not arrest her in front of me. I was all she had now."

Eleven

Y OU LOOK TIRED," Shepherd said, getting up from the hard bench. "Come, let me show you one of my favorite corners of the city," and he offered her a hand.

"Thanks for being here," she said, turning toward him. "I didn't think . . . I mean after so many years . . . that it would still . . ." She fell silent.

"I know," he said, and for some reason she believed he did.

As they walked slowly back toward the street, Anna, recalling an old habit, peered into the dank, gloomy basement: the concierge's apartment. She recognized the heavy, dark furniture which overwhelmed the tiny bedroom. The lace bedspread had not been changed since Anna's childhood. The crucifix with its withered bouquet still hung above the enormous bed. And, tacked to the faded floral wallpaper, an old photograph. A young man, handsome in the dark, romantic way of the times, gleaming hair slicked back, eyes flashing at the pretty woman who held a baby in her lap. "My parents and me," Anna pointed out to Shepherd.

The concierge's apartment was dark. She did not try the doorbell. Would the old woman's eyes locate Anna in the stylishly nonchalant American? She was not prepared to find out.

"This is something I haven't found anywhere else," she turned to Shepherd. "This loyalty across so much time and distance." Why should she care if Shepherd regarded her former countrymen as paid thugs posing as municipal policemen who thrived on wrecking others' lives and possessions? She had come back to claim her old country. She cared. "In America," she pressed on, "people's lives are like revolving doors. Experiences and possessions piled in crazy heaps on top of each other. Don't you think?" she asked, but did not wait for an answer. "Think of Washington or New York! The haunted look of those suddenly on the outside. When people lose a position, they know they are saying goodbye to friends, stature, a way of life. For these people," she said with a nod toward the concierge's apartment, "humanity is all there is. The bonds are lifelong here simply because they keep people sane. Consumption, ambition, the prospect of a brighter future," she shrugged, "are not available diversions."

He said nothing but opened the car door for her.

Once back inside Shepherd's car, she felt a strange lightness. The ghosts of the past, as well as any present shadows, seemed out of place in that smooth German machine. Motion gave them the illusion of freedom. She had begun to like their silences. It gave her the chance to revive in her memory each house, each tree and news vendor they passed. She twisted her head to find the green villa where she had once labored to bend her body into pliées and arabesques. But she couldn't find the spot where it had stood. Or perhaps it was gone, replaced by something new?

They drove past the church where she had spent some of her childhood's most intimate moments. It was still as worn and weathered as an old shoe, though now surrounded by an army of dreary high-rise apartment buildings. A cityscape from Gary, Indiana. Did little girls still breathe their confessions with the same fervor, she wondered, inside that damp, candlelit nave. "Bless me father, for I have sinned . . ."

She recalled the musty smell of the church, the stale breath of the priest as he mumbled her penance through the confessional's grille. The elation she felt walking out of the dark into a chilly late afternoon.

Her childhood Catholicism had the whispered urgency of an illegal faith. During her parents' imprisonment, when she no longer lived in the family's apartment, she often returned to this church. Her godmother taught her a special prayer to the Mother of God. If repeated with sufficient frequency and conviction, it was almost guaranteed to return a captive to his family. At the time, Anna was sure her prayers had played a part in her parents' release.

She had loved those nuns in their gray sweaters and shapeless skirts. The State no longer allowed them to wear their habits. Their eyes had a shine, however; their pale, unpowdered faces had a glow, as though lit up by a secret others were not privy to, which set them apart. She remembered a Maria and a Teréz, bony women who always seemed to be out of breath. There were so many families who needed their services. But they were always eager to get on with the catechism. And one by one, they had vanished. Deported? Arrested? Something worse? Anna had never

forgotten their crystal-hard devotion, their cool, sure hands
on hers.

They crossed the bridge leading to the Margit Island.
This green patch between the two banks of the Danube was
where the city fled to stretch its legs and breathe. In the days
before Hungary became a land where profit, enterprise, and
luck are meant to play no part, they had come to gamble.
Shepherd pulled into a space in front of the copper-colored
new Thermal Hotel. Blocking the hotel entrance were
a cluster of stocky, ruddy-complexioned East Germans.
Wrapped in shiny brown vinyl overcoats, to Anna they
looked like so many Mars Bars. They quivered with amuse-
ment, savoring a hilarious anecdote. Then, suddenly sober,
they stepped to one side, careful not to brush Anna and
Shepherd.

Shepherd steered her toward a stone bench.

"Why has no one ever pointed out the health benefits of
living in a police state?" he asked. "Have you ever noticed
how much more time people spend out in the bug-free fresh
air here than in the decadent West?" She smiled and said,
"Why is it that you don't strike me as someone who could
devote a lifetime to negotiating shipments of Hungarian
salami for American hi-tech? If that's an accurate job de-
scription of a Commercial Attaché?"

"I happen to like good Hungarian salami," he said defensively. "And they happen to appreciate our computers. So
everybody gets something." He shrugged. "It's not a bad
job. You meet rather interesting people along the way. People in the media think anything else is dull and plodding. I
don't happen to agree," he said flatly.

"It's just that there is something," she began, "I don't
quite know how to put this—something too deliberately—

you know, forgive the expression, laid back, about you. I mean, most diplomats do their best to look the opposite of laid back. They work on looking as though they had a lot up their sleeve. Unfortunately, they can't share any of it with you. You, on the other hand . . ." He avoided her gaze and looked down on the hard December ground. "You have perfected the opposite role. Why?" she asked with a mischievous smile.

He laughed, but an edge of awkwardness had crept into that laugh. It was his first unstudied gesture. "The checkered career of any survivor of five administrations. From Rusk to Schultz. A wide range of masters to please," he said, looking off again. "Anyway, we'd both better stop stealing our employers' time." He rose to his feet. "I'll take you back to the hotel."

"Thanks for being with me. It made it easier. I'm not sure why. But it did."

"Any time."

"Christopher," she had never called him by his name before. The afternoon sun was at his back, and its pale rays shot through his thinning hairline. "Would you kiss me?" she said. "Please." Almost obediently, he took her in his arms. Their lips met softly at first, and then with a hunger that grew and nourished itself until both of them pulled away, surprised and slightly breathless. He ruffled her short hair and she rubbed her cheek against the soft tweed of his jacket. "Just don't say anything," she said. "Anything sensible, that is. Just be my friend."

"I already am," he said, his voice lower than before. His tone had a ring of resignation. It occurred to her their friendship had not been part of his own calculation.

Twelve

THE KETTLE'S SHRIEK stirred him from behind his typewriter. He had been stuck on the same paragraph for the past hour. Though his section of the magazine went to bed the following day, his mind kept wandering. "I'll write you from Budapest," his daughter had said on the phone. Her tone was as nonchalant as if she had said, "I'll call you from Bridgehampton." Alex Bator knew better. Knew this was not just one more trip for his daughter, who seemed to spend more time in planes than on the ground.

He walked slowly toward the noisy kettle in his small kitchen and thought, Maybe the time has come. He had never really believed in his family's new-found security. Purchased at a high price, this new life had been a gamble at best. When the time came, he knew he would be able to deal with them, Laci Andor and the rest. In the composed way he had dealt with them before. Besides, Alex knew he had an advantage. He was not nearly so attached to life, not even this present one, as other men.

But his daughter had no such experience. Anna did not

understand that authority could put a pious face on criminal acts. The trouble was, she *thought* she understood. He knew better.

How long had she been gone? One week, two? A sign of age, he supposed, this imprecision about time. He sighed deeply and poured boiling water over two bags of Earl Grey tea. This was Julia's ritual, which Alex performed blindly, loyally, but never without thinking of her. And once again he was struck by the absurdity of his having survived her.

He looked out the window at the snow-blanketed Central Park below. For once, it did not look like a threatening no-man's-land between two opposing camps. The Park was as picturesque as a Currier and Ives lithograph, with tiny smudges of color, children throwing snowballs. He could still appreciate beauty. A Rembrandt portrait still moved him.

He carried the tea things back to the living room on a silver tray. But that *Madonna*, the one in the corner over the sun-bleached, stuffed chair, he had never been affected by her beauty. She was too insipid, with her moist eyes and limpid smile. The portrait may have been the work of a member of the da Vinci School, but surely a member in not very good standing. Of course, there was no question of parting with a portrait weighed down by those associations. The *Madonna* had hung in every one of the Bator homes since . . . well, since everything began to change for them.

A comrade named Kovago had heard the story of how Alex's father had once tried to buy his son's life with that painting. Kovago had a special loathing for the SS Oberführer who had once accepted the elder Bator's treasure with a broad grin. Kovago had been tortured by the same

lover of art in the basement of what is again a popular
Budapest restaurant. Kovago had gone to the trouble of
plowing through the rubble left behind when the Nazi hastily cleared out of his headquarters. Whatever he was looking
for, he found the *Madonna*. Kovago seemed surprised and
disappointed when Alex's eyes failed to light up at the sight
of her. "Thanks for your trouble," was all Bator had managed by way of gratitude. Of course, it was not as much the
Madonna as the memories it stirred up.

But never for long. For Bator had more or less mastered
the art of locking out memories. Curiosity and nostalgia
were viruses he had long ago purged from his system. No
regrets, no yearning for what was or might have been stirred
his blood the way they did his daughter's. What was she
after, really? Alex, who did not fear many things, was afraid
of her romantic curiosity about the past.

He feared all those emotions of hers. He could practically feel them ricocheting off the walls in her presence. He
sipped his tea and thought, Julia was right. Maybe I don't
really know myself, much less others. He reflected on this
without remorse, with relief, almost; he had never had what
is commonly called an inner life, not the way others seemed
to. He stopped sharing his experiences, doubts, feelings with
anyone long ago.

History, a high-sounding word for a string of squalid
moments, had relieved him of the burden of "self-knowledge." At each juncture of his life, he had been rescued from
himself by a crisis of "historic dimensions." Party jargon,
that. The International Brigade. The German Occupation.
The Soviet Occupation. Prison. Each coinciding with his
youth, maturity, midlife—those well-advertised crossroads

in a man's life. He had simply counted on time to pass, and to do its work. Meanwhile, he had effectively locked life out.

The self-discipline required for this performance he mastered early. How old was he when he pulled that stunt at the horse show? Probably no more than seven. A week earlier he had broken out with a bad case of the measles. Hideous red spots erupted on his face, his body. His mother was fretting too much, as usual; of course she forbade him to ride. But the boy had been training for months for this event. On the day of the show, Alex sneaked into his mother's dressing room. He caked his spotted face with her thick powder, pulled his riding hat low over his eyes. Dressed in his riding costume, he announced to his parents he was much better. He hadn't calculated on rain, however. He'd never forget the expression of horror on his mother's face as streaks of makeup ran down his face to reveal bright red measles spots. By then he had already cleared his hurdle. His mother wouldn't let him stay long enough to collect the ribbon.

The only life he had really believed in was his daughter's. For Anna, he had come to this country. And now she had chosen to return to Budapest. There was nothing he could do; she had left him as helpless as a child.

There was so much of the old Julia in Anna, Julia before the fight trickled out of her. Before her voice turned tremulous. She had given up on him toward the end, but he couldn't help that. He felt himself withdraw deeper and deeper into himself, especially after the trip to Paris four years ago. Julia died a couple of years later. The cause of death was pneumonia, but in fact she had simply lost interest in leaving her bed.

He and Laci had met by the kiosk on the rue de Rennes. "What do you need me for?" Alex had asked his old comrade. "I'm no use to you. I'm not a Right Thinker!" And Laci, looking so shabby and out of place on that bright spring day in the middle of a crush of kids jostling their way to the Sorbonne and the neighborhood Lycées, Laci had said, "It's better to be *wrong* with the Party than *right* outside of it!" (Laci was such a plagiarist, Alex thought. Subsequently, he had read that Santiago Carrillo had said the same thing once.) Laci had also become a man of steel. Christ, what do you expect after all those years? And what he had done to Rajk and the others, Alex included. Rajk, so plainly innocent, talked into confessing to treason. A sort of dress rehearsal of Alex's own case.

So, Laci would not hear of Alex's divorce from the Party. But Alex was old, and until Anna started her sentimental talk of Budapest, until then . . . Well, he thought they might be done with him. Let him grow old looking at this park, so blessedly far from the woods, the fields, and the country houses of his youth.

He missed Julia now with a sharp pain like a wound. Though he couldn't bring himself to talk to her at the end, he never would have survived the camp without her. She had saved his life. When he looked around Budapest or what was left of it, he wondered why she had bothered. The bridges had all been blown into the ice floes of the hateful river. And everywhere Alex heard the cries of children, searching the lunar landscape of bombed buildings for a mother or a father. He didn't have to look for his parents. He was not allowed the feeble hope of not knowing exactly what had happened to them.

Alex Bator would never have made a move to save himself. He was basically a passive man, this much self-knowledge he possessed. Being passive entailed fewer risks. His dignity was never unbuttoned. He let things happen to him. People came to him and made him offers. Laci. Julia. The boy who drove the camp delivery truck. It was all the boy's idea to get him out of the camp at Kistarcsa. Why were these memories assaulting him? Anna's trip had sprung them loose: her naive and misguided search.

Thirteen

WHAT BROUGHT YOU HERE, Laci?" Alex had asked one night, when the clatter of machine guns was too close for either man to sleep. Alex and Laci lay side by side on mattresses spread around the floor of the Barcelona school gymnasium, their barracks. An idle, late night question Alex would regret for the rest of his life.

Alex had signed up with the International Brigades aimlessly, at loss for a purpose. He was putting off life for a year. His mother's suffocating concern with how his life was going or not going was also a spur.

Alex didn't play the hero in Spain. Mostly, he drove truckloads of volunteers, ragged idealists from Stuttgart and San Francisco, from one crumbling barricade to the next.

But things had happened to him there. He could still conjure up some of it. The hundreds of bare arms, clenched fists pounding an invisible enemy. The singing and the marching in step to the *Internationale*. So much stronger stuff than the Catholic Church in which he had been scrupulously raised. He also spent a lot of time sitting in cafés with sculptors, journalists, and vagrants. They smiled at the sight of wine spilling on tables that trembled from approaching artillery fire. Their faces were ashine with male pride.

From Spain, Alex Bator observed the countries whose self-proclaimed commitment to decency he had cherished. Britain, France, and far-off America sent only their hungriest idealists and reporters. Germany and Italy parachuted their soldiers and pilots. They wore white overalls over their uniforms but swastikas sometimes poked out from under them. The sight sickened him.

He took in the grotesque Goya landscape: the columns of retreating humanity stumbling blindly over open-mouthed corpses. And he stopped thinking of the Civil War as a sporting event. He took home to Budapest a single sound: the cry of an abandoned child, piercing and hopeless.

And a name: Laci Andor. He remembered how Laci had first kept his distance. They were both in their early twenties. But Andor was painfully callow, with the stoop of a man much older, who spent his early years bent over the soil. His complexion was scarred by childhood diseases left untreated. Alex was keenly aware of his own attributes. His finely chiseled features in silver-framed photographs adorned his mother's dressing table, as well as the nightstand of one of Budapest's great beauties. His high forehead and thick mane of black hair earned him the nickname "Spaniard," long before he volunteered for the Brigades. Laci spoke a rough peasant's Hungarian. Bator diverted the company with anecdotes in three or four languages.

At first Laci just listened to those late night ramblings about the places, the people, the music, and the books which formed the bricks and mortar of Alex's life of privilege. Alex

didn't much care what his countryman—lying on the
ground, his head propped up by his rolled-up jacket, a cigarette perpetually stuck to his lower lip—thought of him.

Until the night he whispered into the dark, "Laci, what
brought you here, anyway?", Alex hadn't paid him the least
attention.

"More a question of what didn't hold me back," Laci had
answered, drawing on his cigarette, which glowed red in the
dark. "No job. Haven't had one in years. Can't even vote in
my own proud parliamentary state. Haven't got any property, y'see. My name's not even my own. My mother's
boyfriend didn't feel like marrying her when I was born.
What else didya wanta know?"

"I wasn't prying. Just interested, that's all."

"Well, the word was out in my neighborhood . . . not
a part of Pest you frequent . . . about this war," said Laci.
"It was a chance to do something other than burn up about
cases like mine. A chance to throw more than words at the
bastards who keep me unfit for society. This is the only
place you can actually do something about all that. For
now . . ."

In their nocturnal confidence, Laci told Alex about his
early life. He and his mother had moved from one muddy
village to the next, looking for work that did not exist. They
sometimes slept on the branches of trees. Laci was seven
years old when his mother gave him his first pair of shoes,
scuffed and far too big, but shoes. His mother was only
forty-five, but looked like his grandmother.

"The Communists are the only ones with a plan," Laci
whispered, "and with discipline. The Social Democrats, they
wanta please everybody. They don't wanta step on no one's

toes. So you can keep your thousand hectares of arable land; the rest of us will go on plowin' it for you. Well, that ain't what I want. Or what these people are getting massacred for."

The blacked-out windows of the school rattled as the bombers cut through the night sky. Laci's voice became more urgent. "There were only eight of us," he told Alex of his first meeting with members of the clandestine Budapest Communist Party. "All hush-hush. You needed passwords to get past the front door. I guess I wouldn't be here to tell the tale otherwise. But the people! Young, beautiful, like I never seen before. I didn't feel like a leper no more."

Alex dozed off before dawn. Laci was still murmuring about the people. Thinking back now, he thought Laci must have perceived some weak spot in Alex's all but flawless guise even then. For in the days that followed, Laci seldom left Alex's side, carrying on about the People over the drone of bombers overhead.

Fourteen

THROUGHOUT his long professional life, Christopher Shepherd had not been a man to lose sight of the task at hand for long. Lately, though, habit had replaced genuine enthusiasm for his job. He kept waiting for the buzz of excitement the approach of a new case once brought him. But the old feeling eluded him, as more and more he allowed his mind to drift to a dilapidated farmhouse thick with wisteria, just north of Aix-en-Provence. He'd caught a glimpse of it the summer before and wondered if it was still for sale.

When the haze of these daydreams, induced by boredom and malaise, lifted, he realized it was useless to spin visions of a different life. Three white linen suits, perfectly cut, and the manners that went with them, were the sum total of his inheritance. All that remained of his father's lifetime of devotion to his Ashville, North Carolina, congregation.

Anna had burst in on his well-ordered life with unexpected exuberance. His habit of reserve, however, was as deeply ingrained as the lines on his brow. He had been emotionally dormant for so long, he was convinced that was the way he liked it. It certainly made his job much easier.

A gentle stirring of his senses had begun. Even he could not completely deny that. He began to look forward to her somewhat breathless phone calls, brief eruptions of light in his dry routine. "Comrade Bator calling," she would say in a thick accent. "Commercial Attaché Shepherd is needed for some agitation and propaganda work. Promptly please."

"So what did you do to earn your outrageous salary today?" he would query.

"Interviewed the head of the Central Bank of the People's Republic. On audio cassette. That's what Comrade Fekete has reduced me to. Radio. I'll soon be forgotten in TV land. I wonder if she's in CBS's pay."

"What did he have to say . . . your banker?"

"Are you debriefing me or what?"

"Just trying to keep you honest."

"Actually he told me he'd rather I didn't rhapsodize too much about how healthy this economy is, compared to the others in the Soviet Bloc. Fears too much attention from us may spell the doom of Hungary's quiet experiment in free enterprise socialism. Goulash communism, he calls it. Not to worry, I told him. Other than my father and my three-year-old daughter, I don't know too many people who listen to these riveting afternoon radio interviews."

"Anybody else lined up today?"

"Only you."

Sometimes, they went for walks through the bare forests of Zugliget on the outskirts of Budapest. These walks made him feel more a part of the fabric of a society he had until now observed closely, yes, but from the outside, gazing in. Zugliget was the escape of other couples, squeezed by a shortage of space and privacy in the city's cramped, multigenerational apartments.

Anna and Christopher strolled among these couples, exchanged smiles of complicity with them, pretended they were like them. Anna liked watching Shepherd's unself-conscious grace, his easy command of his tall, spare body. She liked the way he had begun to notice others. "That woman," he said, "the one on the bench. Quite amazing . . . her legs. Matched only by her vanity. She must be freezing," he said, pulling Anna toward himself roughly with one arm. She laughed at the incongruity of this proper man's keen appreciation of good legs. She basked in his slow transformation.

"Where shall we go?" he asked her without preamble one chilly afternoon. She met his look without blinking. He took her hand and they walked slowly back to his car. In their customary silence, they drove to his apartment.

He slipped off her trenchcoat and kept his fingertips lightly resting on her shoulders. She raised her mouth to his, and they kissed with the fullness of sudden release. "Lovely," he whispered, as if handed a gift. "I . . . want . . . you." His voice had an unusually rough grain to it. His fingertips grazed her throat and the soft skin left exposed by the blouse. His lips traveled from her eyes downward, covering her in a dreamlike web of featherlight kisses. Anna felt a warmth radiate through her body like a balm. As she held him tightly, she could see the city beneath them. No shadowy corners, no uniforms or barbed wire scarred the serenity of the Danube weaving its way through the heart of Budapest. She held him as if in his arms, she could hold the past which she both needed and feared, at bay.

"I know so little about you," she whispered. "It's a little bit frightening, how much I want to share with you," she said.

"Yes, I know," he breathed, gently stroking her naked breasts. He stepped back to look at her. "I've imagined this a hundred times you know," he said, pulling her urgently toward him.

"Oh," she sucked in her breath. "Yes. Touch me like that."

Their passion seemed miraculously calibrated to each other's needs. There was no coyness, no holding back between them. No promises had been made. They made love for one reason; the best of all reasons, because they wanted to. But it was as though they had been together before; their bodies seemed to possess a memory of their own. Sometimes gentle, then, suddenly, demanding and impatient, their movements seemed in perfect harmony. "You feel wonderful," she said between deep kisses which only nourished her hunger for more of him. "Tell me how I can make you feel wonderful."

"I don't have to," he murmured, lightly stroking her belly. "You already know."

Fifteen

SPINDLY TUFTS OF steam curled up from the green surface of the pool, which smelled unpleasantly of sulfur. The Lukacs Baths were teeming with the faithful, who performed their careful breaststrokes with the solemnity of a religious ritual. The swimmers' large heads glowed pink from the bracing winter air; their bodies shone white and glutinous under the heated water. These were the habitués of the Lukacs. They were men of substance whose solid flesh was only the outward reminder of their weight and position in society: Party elders, editors of literary and political journals, a baritone from the state opera, and the doctor who had prolonged their combined years of service to the State. They were drawn by more than the therapeutic benefits of the city's favorite Turkish baths.

As the swimmers gently spread the bubbling green water before them, they engaged in a low, nearly uninterrupted flow of conversation. The Lukacs is the one place in Budapest where you can freely trade ideas and gossip. The corpulent regulars assume that neither Moscow nor Washington has yet devised a way of monitoring waterborne conversations.

In this pool, Christopher Shepherd, whose job it was to be on top of such things, first picked up a tremor of something. His instincts for distinguishing between the real and the rumor told him to keep swimming. Keep listening. Shepherd was a crawl man. The breaststroke was not his idea of real swimming. But he was sure he had heard three words correctly as they floated back to him across the malodorous water: "Repercussions," "tank movements," and "Solidarity." He slowed his usual pace to match the swimmers'. Shepherd found the Magyar tongue the most elusive of the half dozen he had mastered on tours from Kabul to Nicosia. But, unlike his colleagues at the embassy (and unbeknownst to them), he spent much of his free time, earphones clapped to his head, listening to Hungarian language tapes. For this part of his job, the mastering of unyielding languages, continued to engage him in the old way. On this first day of winter at the Lukacs, his linguistic efforts paid off.

The two swimmers, like a pair of ancient crocodiles in some steaming jungle river, reached the shore. Shepherd continued his laps uninterrupted. His ears, however, were pricked up in perfect concentration, able to filter out all sounds save the low murmurs of the pair. The two men heaved their large lumps of flesh from the water onto the moist deck. Shepherd heard them padding toward the glassed-in area that led to the dressing rooms. He continued swimming. He would have to return.

"Aha," Anna said to him with a bright smile one week later. "It hasn't taken you long to find the real center of

power in the city." She pushed off from the side, cut
through the water with strokes as clean as a sailboat. The
Lukacs had been her childhood's safe, crowded pond. "I was
four years old," she turned back to face him, "when I was
first initiated into the rites of the Lukacs." Shepherd caught
up with her and now they were swimming in rhythm. "They
strapped a canvas belt around my tummy and hooked a
fishing pole-like contraption into it. Someone held the pole
above the water while I flapped my arms and legs in what
I imagined to be a perfect imitation of the breaststroke." The
two of them were alone in the water. Anna hooked her legs
around his and touched her cheek to his wet shoulder. "Oh,
it's so easy being with you!" His smile was distracted. "I
made sure no one was in the pool to witness my humiliation," she continued, "but, of course, good old Uncle Zoli,"
she shook her head, "Zoli never missed a day at the Lukacs.
Then or now, I gather. He took it all in with great glee. I
never forgave him."

"Zoli?" Shepherd asked.

"Not my real uncle. An honorary one. Better known to
you as Zoltán Boros. Private secretary and spiritual guru to
Chairman Kadar." Anna swung her legs over the side in one
motion. Shepherd, still in the water, did not move. "One of
my father's oldest friends. They were classmates at the same
fancy boys' school. Hundreds of years ago. Zoli, from what
I hear, was the irresistible butt of every playground prank.
He was short, gawky, and much too smart. Being Jewish
was not a plus. My father got a lot of bloody noses standing
between Zoli and the genteel thugs on the soccer field. That,
I guess, is the secret behind their lifetime bond. In spite of
some fairly obvious differences since those days. Is this bor-

ing you?" she asked, wondering why his face was stripped of all expression.

"No. No, not at all," he said impatiently, as if emerging from a dream. "Your family's story continues to fascinate me. Go on." He did not look at her, but eased himself out of the pool and threw on a terrycloth robe. Anna's Uncle Zoli was one of the two swimmers whose conversation he had attempted to follow during his last visit to the Lukacs.

"Zoli served as a witness for the prosecution," Anna continued, "during my parents' trial. Quite a pragmatic fellow, as you can see. He stayed scrupulously loyal to Moscow throughout the fifties. In '56 I don't think he touched the Freedom Fighters with a barge pole. My father used to say how lucky the Party was to have him on its side. If you see him, he'll remind you of a different incarnation. A shifty cardinal, oiling around the Vatican, say, under Julian II. Or maybe in white silk tights, carefully picking his way around Versailles, under Louis XIV. There is something of the timeless courtesan about Zoli."

"C'mon, let's get dressed," Shepherd spoke at last. "I'm famished." Moments later, their hair still damp but their cheeks glowing with health, they walked across the bare little park surrounding the crumbling Turkish baths. "Look," Anna pointed toward the gold-lettered marble slabs, some dating as far back as the sixteenth century, testimony of grateful beneficiaries of the Lukacs's waters. "Someday there will be one from Zoltán Boros. With profound thanks for helping him survive a dozen purges, a revolution, and a counterrevolution. Each time they came for him, he was here doing his laps."

"Anna," Shepherd dropped a hand on her arm, "it

would mean a great deal to me, if you were to resume your old friendship with Boros." It was a voice she had not yet heard: dead serious, implying far more than he was saying.

"Oh God," she sighed, "you're a spook, aren't you?" But still he said nothing.

"Uncle Zoli is anything but a dull man." She shrugged. "I wanted to get in touch with him anyway. See what's happened to the old operator."

With an arm around her shoulder, he turned Anna toward himself. He planted a soft kiss on the tip of her nose and flashed an uncharacteristic, broad smile. She slipped an arm through his. For a split second, she wondered if she would ever mean very much to him.

Sixteen

THE LAST TIME she saw Zoli, she had been wearing a Young Pioneers red kerchief around her neck. Red was the only color in the streets of Budapest in the fifties. Pinks, greens, and yellows had been washed away in a flood of khaki and brown. Long lines of people, the color of slush, waited for buses and trams, for brown bread and bruised apples. Only the wearer's shape made a difference to the unisex trousers and coats, the only available choices at the Corvin People's Department Store. In those days, clothes were meant to cover, not fit.

She remembered waving to him during a May Day parade, proud of this link to someone who stood just behind the barrel-chested front line. Zoli had merely winked back at her. Did he enjoy those parades as much as she had, secretly? The music that reached all the way from the roots of your hair down into your shoes. Those songs about looking ahead, never backward. Forward! She merged into a sea of eyes, noses, lips moving in unison. Obliterated as a separate, troublesome individual. Ground into the fine dust of the people. The martial sound of the *Internationale*. And all of them dwarfed by those gigantic portraits. Stalin, Lenin, Marx, Rákosi. Byzantine icons in procession for a powerful and thrilling new faith.

The only parade Anna had ever seen before was on St. Stephen's Day. The priests turned out in all their gold finery, waved incense, and carried Stephen's withered arm in a glass casket. That parade was nine hundred years old and not nearly as stirring as this new one. This was just like being in a play. But she could never admit this to her parents. At dinner that night she grumbled about being rounded up along with the other idiots in her class.

She sat now in the peppermint-and-white snackbar of the Intercontinental Hotel and thought, these people don't look at all as if they march in May Day parades. The glass-enclosed snackbar faced the Danube and could have been in Austria or Italy. It was a scene from well west of the barbed wire, the watchtowers, and the dogs ready to bark. Perhaps not from Vienna or Rome, but a restaurant in the provinces. A place where the customers aped the styles they imagined to be still raging in the big cities.

Everything was just one shade off. The hairstyles were an inch too long, and too puffed up, the skirts a nuance too short. But colors there were in abundance. Garish lime greens fought with canary yellows for attention. And the customers' faces looked relaxed, unhurried. No one seemed to mind the slow service. She wondered if sloppy service was still a positive sign here, a sign the secret police were not interested in this particular institution.

Next to her, two rumpled, androgynous youths, with long, stringy hair, wearing worn blue jean jackets, were locked in intense conversation. A curtain of smoke was the only thing separating them. Where were the furtive glances, the military set features of her childhood? Expressions had matched the cut of people's clothes in those day. Today the coffeeshop's loudspeakers hummed Chicago's "If You Leave Me Now."

Whiling away the afternoon in a café would have been deemed a subversive act in her childhood. As for loudspeakers, they were always turned up to their maximum capacity (wasn't that an expression from the workers' lexicon?) and exhorted you to UNMASK MANIFESTATIONS OF NATIONALISM AND CHAUVINISM! ALL WORK URGENTLY NEEDED! CLOSE RANKS AROUND THE PARTY! AGAINST THE ENEMY!

There was really no escape: every tree, each tobacconist, no matter how dilapidated, was plastered with a slogan. ETERNAL VIGILANCE! they had screamed at her, robbing her of a real, pastel-hued childhood.

In the Hungary of her memory, no corner was slogan-proof. Her mother told of looking up at the ceiling from her hospital bed in the labor ward giving birth to Anna. Though her vision was blurred by oncoming contractions, she made out the letters on the green ceiling: FOR A MARRIED WOMAN TO GIVE BIRTH IS A DUTY! FOR AN UNMARRIED WOMAN TO GIVE BIRTH IS A GLORY!

"So, little Anna hasn't forgotten us!" Zoltán Boros, engulfed in jowls, eyes protruding and alert, folded her into an exuberant bear hug. Anna, unexpectedly moved by his enthusiasm and by all the things that tied them into a common knot, pressed her cheek against the rough folds of his face. "My God," Zoli said, unabashedly inspecting her, "Barbara Walters must be worried!" He looked immensely pleased with his command of American esoterica. Anna could not repress a smile.

"Zoli, you haven't changed at all," she lied. In fact, only the leonine-shaped head resisted the years, which had clearly alternated between too much good living and too much of the opposite. Boros's shapeless, wide nose glowed a conspicuous red in a face the color of lead. Tufts of coarse gray hair poked out of his eyebrows, nostrils, and ears. He still wore his worker's half coat, which she now recalled had been his trademark. Political expediency seemed to dictate this flaccid-limbed man's every choice. He now offered her one of his stubby little Hungarian cigarettes. Anna declined, but Boros lit one and filled the air with dark, foul-smelling rings. Even Brezhnev openly displayed his preference for Marlboros, she thought. Why does Zoli still feel obliged to smoke cigarettes that peel away on his tongue?

"You've made us all proud, Annikam," he said, drawing hard on his little brown butt. Everything about him, she observed, his eyes, his cheeks, even his feet, seemed to sag toward the floor. Everything, she felt sure, except his mind. "You look the perfect advertisement for the Land of Opportunity," he said with only a trace of irony. She was not sure how to respond to the bemused expression on his face. He was beginning to disarm her with that look of vague superiority. "You are American now," his look told her, "and of the most insulated sort. You no longer fit into this world. You are not, therefore, qualified to penetrate our more complex motives." She was determined not to allow him this distance. She wanted some of his complexity.

"The Lady with the olive branch," Anna said, pointing behind Boros's stooped shoulder to the Gellert Hill, capped by an enormous muscular female, the memorial to the Soviet Army of Liberation. "So she still owns the skyline?" she asked, with a goading smile.

"Why not?" Zoli shrugged. "There's plenty of room up there."

"Do people remember, I wonder," she pursued, "that the Winged Lady had been commissioned by the Old Regent? As a memorial to his son. The one shot down by the 'Liberators'?"

"Dear Anna, your parents must have told you," Zoli's tone was irresistibly avuncular, "that this is not a place where a good memory is a useful gift." He smiled pleasantly.

"There has never been much discussion about the past in our family," she said, and wondered if Zoli knew this. Did he understand that was why she was back?

Boros signaled for the harried waitress, who smiled in recognition and continued to ignore them. Anna was overwhelmed by the feeling that this man had much of her family's past at his tobacco-stained fingertips. She had no idea how or where to begin. She felt inept and clumsy facing this old master of subterfuge. As an American reporter she had mastered other talents: speed, authority, and bluster. A stranger to caution, she fought back a dozen questions.

How, she wondered, had he survived those purges? And how could he reconcile his faith, if faith there still was, to the grim record?

She knew from her father that Zoli had once challenged the Sorbonne's complacent ideas on both Montaigne and Proust. That he was as conversant with Mahler as he was with Marx. Zoli had also seen the Party grow from a tight fistful of renegades on the run, changing names and hideouts weekly, into the Keeper of the Prison State. And now, the present, more benevolent version. How did this infinitely worldly and most European of men sleep at night, with all that on his back?

"Two espressos," he told the chubby waitress, who pushed a dirty rag around their marble-topped table. She soon plunked down two tiny cups of the black liquid. Anna knocked back hers as she had seen others around her do. The coffee felt like a flame sliding down her throat.

"Your father?" he asked. "Is he well? I was desolated by the news of your mother's death. Four, five years ago?"

"Two and a bit. Yes. She was never very strong," she said quietly, not yet able to approach the subject without a break in her voice. "My father still works harder than most people I know. And is among the most patriotic Americans. In part from gratitude, I suppose, for the way we've been treated."

"Your father is among the bravest men I have ever known." His tone was even, unshaded by innuendo. "Always was." He signaled the waitress for two more cups of the poisonous black liquid. "Even in short pants. He had this thing about bullies. God, I'd run till my sides split, not even turning around to look. He'd stay to get his face smashed. When they shouted 'Yid,' he saw red. He was always outnumbered, of course. That's why he took up fencing." He spoke matter-of-factly, as though he and Anna had covered this ground before. Anna tried not to look too avid, not to show the weight she attached to each word he tossed effortlessly in her direction. "Fencing, at least, gave him the chance to take them on. One at a time. He became one of our best, you know. In those days, you could still settle an argument with foils. Not legally, of course. Your father turned Budapest into Richelieu's Paris with all his duels. But it didn't last. Foils weren't much good against pistols and jackboots." Boros leaned back, pushed his cup away.

"He's still a brave man," Anna said, anxious not to stray too far. "But these days his biggest battles involve beating the gentleman from *Newsweek* on the number of non-attributable quotes from highly placed United Nations sources. Not much of a challenge for him. Not compared to . . ." Compared to what? She was not certain, but prayed he would go on.

"The camps or the prison?" he suggested. "Maybe that's why he's such a grateful American. Maybe he's earned his boredom on the East River." Boros sounded as if he were talking not about his old schoolmate, but about himself. His own right to be bored.

"You and Father," she began, aiming for a casual tone, "both set your sights westward, toward Paris and London. Isn't it strange you ended up choosing such . . . well . . . such different paths?" She smiled at him ingenuously.

"Well, well. You don't believe in too much small talk," he said. "Well, you're a reporter, just like him. Deadlines. Always deadlines, huh? Little Anna, I'll let you in on a secret," he leaned toward her conspiratorially. She felt his sour tobacco breath against her cheek. "I'm first and last a Hungarian. And there's not much in between. I can remember things that happened right on this plot of land. Before they poured the cement and franchised it to Intercontinental Hotels. Before the blue-haired American ladies arrived. I saw people standing here looking into this river. The Blue Danube. It was often more red than blue. People with their wrists manacled together so the executioner could save the bullets. One would serve for two. Their crime"—his speech was cut short by a rough eruption of coughing—"their crime was having been part of the most patriotic Jewish community in Europe. The people who made this city the cultural and intellectual center it was becoming. The Kordas, the Soltis, the von Neumanns, and the rest. The smart ones left. The rest, those with too much baggage to move, stayed. And paid." He picked a fleck of tobacco off his tongue and cleared his weary throat. "I joined the Party"; he shrugged. "At least they seemed to offer a new start. A clean break with the past. Oh, I'm not saying we made no mistakes along the way. In those days, our motto was, If you're not with us, you're against us. Now it's, If you're not *against* us, you're *with* us. A big, a huge, difference. You were a child, Anna," He shook his head.

"We lived differently then. It should not come again," he said hoarsely. The mask of bemused detachment slipped. His jaw hung in loose folds and his eyes no longer seemed in focus, but were clouded by an old man's private visions. "Sure. I told them a few things about your parents," he said, reading her thoughts. "I also knew that whatever the AVO wouldn't get from me it would get from someone a lot less concerned about Alex and Julia's welfare. You will never know what it is to live with daily fear," he added simply, in a tone that left no room for discussion.

Anna remembered the first time she had seen the face of fear: the face of Ilonka, her mother's childhood friend. Ilonka was a pretty woman, with curly dark hair, vivid red lips, and an irritating, nervous giggle. Her chief passion was gin rummy, Tuesday and Thursday afternoons. She was also married to one of the country's best-known scientists, a Lenin Prize winner. The couple were coddled by the regime, accorded amazing privileges: a chauffeured Mercedes, a country house by Lake Balatón. Ilonka, with no children of her own, had promised to look after Anna if ever her friend were in trouble.

One day, Anna stood at her doorstep with the AVO officer's bulky figure silhouetted against the dark corridor. "Mommy told them you expected me, Ilonka," Anna said, embarrassed for Ilonka, who seemed to have nothing to say to her. Ilonka just stood there, her eyes as round as cherries; her hands rolled and unrolled a fine linen handkerchief, moist with her own perspiration. "Come in, Anna. I'll give you lunch," she said finally. "And you must tell me where to send you parcels. Food and clothes. Whatever you need." Ilonka spoke in a voice not intended for Anna, but the man in the shadows.

"But, Anna," Zoli interrupted her reverie, "you aren't the only one with questions. Why are you back in Budapest instead of making a big splash in New York? Isn't that where all the other pretty faces bake under klieg lights for millions of dollars? Budapest isn't even covered by Nielsen to my knowledge." Zoli had recovered his old form. Anna concluded he must subscribe to *Variety*.

"Oh, I'll do the obligatory Hungarian miracle story. You know, try to explain why the shops are brimming with such consumer necessities as compact discs and pickled sturgeon, how come the ladies look like Paris last year rather than Vladivostok this year. Why are the jokes more brazen than anywhere else inside the Soviet barracks. And I hope to begin work just as soon as your adorable Comrade Fekete gives me the green light to bring in a TV crew."

"First correction: she is not 'my' Comrade Fekete. I cannot be held accountable for all excesses. She definitely fits that category. As to your story idea, I think you already know the answer." Zoli's face was cracked by his irresistible, conspiratorial smile. "We have become specialists in managing quite nicely under occupations of all sorts. Hundreds of years of it have finely honed our survival instincts. By survival, we mean as pleasantly as possible, of course . . . without calling attention to ourselves. Not like those romantic Poles, who have to beat their chests and chant their Hail Marys loud enough for the Politburo's ears to prick up. We do it differently here," he said, twisting a loose facial fold between his thumb and forefinger. "We use our brains a little bit more."

"So all those terrible jokes about a Hungarian being the guy who gets in the revolving door behind you and gets out ahead of you, all true?"

"Of course. Look at yourself. A dazzling illustration of my point," he said smiling.

"I'm not going to do you the favor of asking what you mean by that. There is something else I would like to do while I am here," Anna said. "The least covered chapter of the Nazi horror. You alluded to this a moment ago . . . The nightmare of the Hungarian Holocaust."

"Ach," Zoli said with a low sigh, "this is not among my very favorite subjects."

"Well, no, but it's a fascinating story. How it could happen so quickly in such a small country, with a pretty good record for tolerance . . . Eichmann at his maximum efficiency."

"Of course. Of course. Maybe for you it's a 'fascinating story.' For me, I don't like to relive it unless I am forced to. Perhaps you can understand . . ." His voice trickled out.

"But it's an important part of the overall history," she pressed on in her determined professional voice. "How these things can happen in such a place. You don't just lose one slice of the population in a country like Hungary . . . people had to know what was going on. . . ."

"Yes, for you this is all history. And I can also imagine in your family this was probably not a big topic," he said, and snapped his finger impatiently at the waitress. Anna felt responsible for his change of mood.

"Well, perhaps there is somebody," he said, digging in his pocket for change. Anna reached for her handbag but he waved her hand away. "Her name is Erzsébet Miklos. That was not her name before, of course. Before her name ended with 'man.' Erzsébet has a much better memory than I do. She does not have as many distractions these days, either. What is more," he was on his feet now, jabbing his short arms into the sleeves of his worn worker's half coat, "she is a talker. If you let her, she will talk your head off." With a sudden surge of energy he bounded out of the coffeeshop, Anna behind him breathlessly trying to keep up. "We will see each other again," he told her on the street. "Of that I have not the slightest doubt." He smiled but this time offered only the brusque wave of a gnarled hand.

Seventeen

"HOW MUCH do you love me?" she shouted into the receiver, and across a continent and an ocean she heard the telephone receiver hit the kitchen floor, and could picture Sarah, arms flung wide, showing her mother just how much.

"That much," Sarah answered, retrieving the telephone once more. "When are you coming home, Mommy?" she asked with a child's infinite adroitness at inflicting guilt.

"Soon, darling, soon. I miss you, too. So much." Mother and daughter made their ritual smacking noises at each other before hanging up. Anna sat for a moment, suspended, waiting for the pain of Sarah's absence to ease. No lover, no husband will ever wield this kind of power over me, she thought, not for the first time. That irresistible, curly-headed tyrant who had, by now, returned cheerfully to her crayons and her Daddy, leaving her limp with longing.

But this is for you too, she thought. I'm here for you, Sarah. So that someday you and I will sit across a table from each other and talk about grandparents and great-grandparents and the jagged path that led them from the Old World to the New. The way I have never done with my mother and father.

There was nothing startling in what she wanted for her daughter. Like most parents, she wanted her to have what she herself did not: a strong sense of herself, a self-esteem based on squarely acknowledging her inheritance. She did not want Sarah to fall between cultures, the way she had. Sarah would not pick up odd bits of this and that society and never be able to claim one as genuinely her own. She would be free of the anxiety of not knowing her own heritage.

"Hello," Anna said in Hungarian after she finished dialing the number Zoli had given her. "My name is Anna Bator."

"Oh, yes," the voice on the other end, seductive and girlish, said after a moment. They made a date to meet for lunch the next day. "Today," Erzsébet Miklos informed her, "I have an appointment at the hairdresser's, and then a fitting at my dressmaker's. Enough excitement for one day." Not so bad, Anna thought, life in a People's Republic.

Anna's hotel room felt very small suddenly. She reached for her raincoat and set off with no particular destination in mind. She fixed Sarah's image firmly on her mental screen. That blue-eyed imp with the smile of an eternal plotter, the future bearer of this rich inheritance. Anna felt an inexplicable rush of energy, stronger and more clear-headed than she had for a long time.

As she walked the streets of her old city, the winter's day fused gradually with her summertime memories. The dull thunk of a ball bouncing off a crumbling wall. The dissonant shouts of children and the rasping symphony of insects in the garden. The city of her childhood. Long before life had become a matter of substituting one form of restlessness for another, for a short while she had known a child's pure sense of well-being here, in the same city that held so many ghosts.

She prowled side streets she had never noticed. She scanned grimy buildings, layered by time and history, now her history. She thought about the empty bustle of her present life: all the playacting that her marriage extracted from her. New York. Its frenetic drive toward what peak? How had she been swept into an elaborate dance, for which she no longer recalled the steps?

She followed an uneven, cobblestoned street that led to the Vorosmarty Square. Across the narrow street, a sudden burst of light cut like a laser through the soft afternoon. Light from the interior of a colorless car. A shape in the semi-dark was outlined for a moment, before the car door shut and the light went out. Anna continued walking. As a child she had known about fear. But that was in a different life, long ago. Anyway, Shepherd, she thought, her friend, was a mere ten-minute walk away. Under the armor of the American reporter, she felt safe.

She settled at last in the faded splendor of the Vorosmarty Coffee House. The aching slowness with which the bureaucratic wheels turned here (she had not yet heard from Comrade Fekete on the subject of either her own crew or three telex machines for the future UNS bureau) had a lulling effect. Anna felt momentarily relieved of the compulsion to be charged either with ambition or purpose. In Budapest, a city of survivors, Anna felt it was sufficient just to be.

She scanned the faces around her. In the pale, lined face of a man partly screened by a newspaper in a cane dispenser, she recognized her father's high forehead. Only her father's eyes were different from this man's. Her father's eyes held every shade of emotion—pride, disappointment, fear, even love—in permanent check, doled them out in precise, meager slices. The slightly Asiatic slant of a woman's eyes, blurred by smoke, she recognized from her own mirror. Most remarkable of all was the universal use of the language which had been her most private code. Hungarian. Everyone spoke the language of her prayers and her curses.

A diminutive couple, she birdlike under a brimmed, felt hat, his once sharp features softened by melancholy, his collar worn but cardboard stiff. This couple matched her private image of Sandor and Klara Bator, the grandparents who did not survive the war.

Anna reached for the *Népszabadság,* the Party organ, left behind on the chair next to hers. From habit, she studied the faces of the group portrait which dominated the skimpy paper's front page. It was the regulation court photograph of the five Communist Party chiefs gathered at Gorbachev's dacha outside Moscow for the purpose of demonstrating the iron bond of their fraternity.

Anna was struck, however, by the strained expression of the lined visage of Janos Kadar. His smile, even given the murky quality of the newsprint, looked to be the result of a painful act of will. Nor was the richly decorated, thin-lipped general who presides over martial law in his native Poland part of the reunion.

She scanned the article entitled "Polish Revisionism" next to the picture. "It is extremely painful," it read, "to see one of the individual fraternal parties fall for the bait of opportunists of various colors." The author struck a note of calculated doom. "Not a single Communist can or will agree with those 'pseudo-theoreticians' who, forgetting the class nature of the Communist movement, propagandize fictitious and deplorable 'models of socialism' and ideas of so-called 'liberalization' of socialism. . . ." The turgid prose rolled on in this inexorable, mind-numbing way.

The litany was as familiar to her as a childhood prayer. She sensed its deliberate obfuscation couched a deeper meaning. It always did. The words explained much about the accompanying portrait, but not enough. A boot had been put to the spade meant to begin the groundwork. But for what? Anna stirred slowly from her lethargy.

Eighteen

LACI'S DECISION, as he later told Alex, was taken one week after he was informed of Anna's second meeting with Shepherd. He made up his mind during his preferred time for matters of this sort: his early morning drive to work.

Barely turning his head, Andor took in the street where his dark blue Mercedes waited. He folded his long frame into the car, which pulled away from the curb in one noiseless sweep.

He settled into the dark blue embrace of the back seat, and sniffed the unmistakable rich smell of the leather upholstery. This car was the single trapping of his office he allowed himself. He cared nothing for clothes. That was obvious from his shapeless suit of synthetic material; a suit Alex would have pronounced hopeless. Andor prided himself on his austerity. He had never had the time for women or food or wine. It was too late now. Nor did he have any conversational topics outside his work. He simply wasn't interested. Not like that schmuck Zoli Boros who, given half a chance, could talk your head off about total irrelevancies. Writers, actors, places Andor had never even heard of. Rubbish. Zoli, he thought, was a weak man. A show-off. Too easily swayed. These days, Zoli was showing signs of a certain cockiness, a certain looseness in his tongue. At the last Central Committee meeting, Zoli had the nerve to stand up and gush sentimentally about the historical and emotional ties linking the Polish and the Hungarian people. Now, of all times. Bastard.

Alone, inside his beautiful car, Andor allowed himself to savor the hard road he had traveled from dirt poor outcast to this. He smiled and parted the opaque curtains that ensured his safe distance from the people. His car passed a pale green building that still bore the marks of stray bullets from '56. He made a mental note to see about that. The fewer reminders, the better. The building looked familiar. He had been inside that building once. St. Joseph's Children's Hospital, the sign read. Of course.

The little girl lying on her pillow, her head flopped to one side, sheet white. Anna Bator had looked like a battered china doll. Twelve children in the same room. They all had that look. As though they didn't have any connection to life, or much interest. Three- and four-year-olds, and none of them made any noise. That was the eerie thing, so many kids and no noise. And there was Alex standing next to Anna's bed, holding her tiny hand in his. Alex standing there, straight as a sentry. But even Alex Bator couldn't control the terror in his eyes.

"They won't tell us what she's got, Laci," he whispered, though the child looked as if gunfire wouldn't stir her. "Look at this sickening rubbish they're spreading in the papers."

Alex unrolled the flimsy newspaper in his pocket. The head-line read: "Imperialist Plot to Kill Children of Working Class."

"Laci, is Anna a child of the working class? Are any of these children? Filthy liars." He was still whispering, but his face had turned a deep red. The flush of rage and panic barely contained. "Nobody wants to tell us what she's got. Laci, you're the only one who can help. Find out what the hell is going on. Please," he said, his voice hardly audible. She really looked pathetic, Andor thought. Those big hazel eyes didn't even see her own father anymore.

"And look at this," Alex said, pointing to a large plate of boiled potatoes and sausages untouched on Anna's night-stand. "This is what they try to feed her. When she can't even open her mouth." Alex's voice was pitched very high and Andor was beginning to feel uncomfortable.

A nurse in a soiled uniform, a sullen look of boredom on her face, strolled by Anna's bed. She picked up Anna's lifeless hand to take her pulse. "Why don't you give her milk?" Alex asked her. "Surely, you can't expect her to eat this farmer's lunch? You must see she can't open her mouth any more." The nurse scowled. "We can't give them milk," she said irritably, "because we haven't got a refrigerator." The nurse picked up the untouched plate. "This was on the menu today." She walked away.

"Laci," Alex pleaded, "this is outrageous. Unless you get this ward a refrigerator, unless you find out what these children have . . ."

"There is no point," Andor spoke softly and evenly, "in threats, Alex. That will get you nowhere. I will look into this matter and call you when I find out."

"Please." Alex's voice was under control again. "We haven't got much time." That much Andor already knew.

He also knew why nearly one hundred children lay limp in their beds, unable to unlock their jaws. For days, he had been trying to repair the damage from an incident that threatened to erupt into a major scandal. But these were hard times. The regime was in its early days. Human mistakes were unavoidable.

The hospital was not at fault. Nor were the doctors who had inoculated one hundred children against whooping cough. Their laboratory technicians had made repeated requests for separate filters for each serum. He had seen the forms himself. "At the present time, we have one filter for all inoculations," it read. "It is impossible to assure the filter's absolute cleanliness when it is used for a range of antitoxins from measles to chicken pox to whooping cough."

The Minister of Health, a comrade rather more interested in her advance in the Party than in matters as trivial as clean filters, sent back a tersely worded memo: "Request denied. Wash the filter properly after each use." The minister's skill at keeping costs down in her department had been held up for praise by Chairman Rákosi in his last address to the Central Committee. The Chairman had big things in mind for her. Until this.

Three-year-old Anna Bator had been inoculated against whooping cough and was now in the grip of an advanced state of tetanus. The serum had been contaminated by an improperly washed filter. Of course, all concerned had been pledged to silence. Andor himself had cooked up the newspaper piece about the "Imperialist Plot to Kill Children of the Working Class." Not an original explanation perhaps, but one that had done the job in the past.

The director of the laboratory who had measured the contaminated serum had already been placed under arrest. Andor and the head of the AVO, Colonel Fodor, had planned a trial, during which the technician would reveal the names of the "plotters." Unfortunately, the man turned out to be spineless. They had found him hanging in his cell in the Fo Street just that morning.

Andor was never slow to grasp an opportunity. He would get his hands on a limited supply of anti-tetanus serum. A friend in the Moscow Health Ministry owed him more than one favor. He would save Anna Bator's life, and maybe one or two others', to allay suspicion.

Andor's car climbed gently up the Gellert Hill to the Citadel. Now she was back, a full-grown woman. A reporter. She hadn't wasted much time getting hold of Zoli. Zoli, the thorn in his side. And this American Commercial Attaché who was no more a commercial attaché than Andor was an astronaut. Anna Bator was seeing a great deal of this man.

For a while after Andor produced the anti-tetanus serum that saved his daughter's life, Alex Bator continued to perform his occasional services with acquiescence. He sold Party-inspired pieces to the magazine and shaded his own articles according to Laci's needs. Andor drew the curtains of his car window together. Well, perhaps this time, he thought, we have something even stronger than serum to induce Alex's return. For Laci thought it was time for his old friend to come home. After all, hadn't Alex been richly rewarded for that long-ago confession they had wrung out of him? Why shouldn't he come home now and help Laci orchestrate what would surely be a difficult public relations job? If Laci knew anything at all about the Western media, he suspected they would go completely berserk over the inevitable resolution to the Polish troubles. He could use a little support from Alex on how to stage-manage this problem. Besides, it had never been Laci's intention to cut Alex completely loose. It was always a matter of time.

Nineteen

I'M ERZSÉBET," the voice, young and breathless, belonged to a woman who, in a softer light, might have passed for middle-aged. "Please call me Bözsi," she said, sitting down across from Anna. Erzsébet had chosen the place for their rendezvous. Anna would have preferred a restaurant where the menu was not translated into English, French, and German. "Shall I order for us both?" Bözsi offered, wide eyes the color of the summer sky beaming flirtatiously at Anna. Her skin was tanned to a golden bronze, carefully lubricated and deeply lined. A great beauty in her day, Anna observed, who has refused to learn how to be anything else.

"I love coming here!" Bözsi enthused at the riotous disorder of the dining room. The waiters, decked out in their traditional peasants' Sunday-best costumes, swirled in their flowing white shirts, velvet vests, and red boots. Every inch of wall and upholstery in the Kalocsa Restaurant was draped with brightly embroidered throws. Tucked inside the chrome-and-marble sheen of the Hilton Hotel, Anna thought the Kalocsa had an oddly synthetic feel, like drinking good wine from a styrofoam cup. "I always pick up *Time* magazine in the lobby." Bözsi said with pride. "It's no more than three weeks dated usually. So many people are afraid to be seen buying them," she whispered in amazement. "I am afraid of nothing!" Then, as if suddenly remembering, Bözsi probed Anna's features with greedy eyes. "So! You are Alex's daughter," her voice had a girl's lilt. She shook her head, making a "Tch, tch" sound of disbelief with her tongue. "Has he grown very old?" she asked in a tone that suggested Bözsi had once been in love with her father.

··"No. He really hasn't. It's unfair the way men don't, isn't it?" Anna asked, realizing too late this was probably the wrong thing to say to a woman of such transparent vanity. "Oh, he's no youngster," she added hastily. "But still nice-looking, I think." She shrugged, vaguely embarrassed. "But then he's my father."

"My God, he was so handsome," Bözsi said, her striking blue eyes ashine. "Of course that was such a long time ago . . . a long, long time . . ." Her voice floated away on its own memories. "I have not seen him since"—she paused—"is it possible? Yes, not since the war." For a split second she dropped the pretty flirt's masquerade and sank into her own age. Then, resisting the gathering melancholy, she straightened up and grabbed Anna's hand. "What a lovely thing you are! Why have you come to Budapest? Other than to meet the famous Erzsébet, of course."

"Yes, to meet the famous Erzsébet." Anna smiled, disarmed by the older woman's childish appetite for flattery. "And also from curiosity about my former home—her history and mine."

"Yes. There is so much here," Bözsi said, hands piously folded on her skin-tight bodice, implying her breasts held a million secrets. "There is not so much of that in New York? We Hungarians love this history . . . the sadness of our destiny. It gives us an excuse to get drunk . . . and to weep." She flashed a gleam of dental gold.

"It's hard to imagine *you* weeping. You have so much spirit," Anna said, "but you have probably lived through quite a few things. . . ."

"Oh yes," Bözsi sighed, a Cheshire cat smile on her lips. "Enough to fill a book or two."

"What was it like then . . . in the worst times? I'm fascinated by this . . ." she asked with a wide-eyed wonder she hoped Bözsi would not easily resist.

"I had an easier time actually than a lot of others . . . because of the sort of person I am," Bözsi said, as if stating the self-evident.

"But still you must have witnessed things . . . heard about them?"

"Oh, I more than *witnessed* things," Bözsi said somewhat archly. "I only meant I am the sort who always lands on her feet. Also I can usually find something to laugh about in every situation. This is my secret to survival. This made things much easier for me than for those who take life too seriously. People like your father, for example."

"My father?"

"Well, yes. For him it was terrible. He was a great snob, you know. After a while he wanted nothing more to do with me. Of course I always knew he would marry a Christian." She showed Anna a still fine profile.

Bözsi's words dropped with such speed and disorder

they left Anna too confused to form a question. And yet she
felt a clarity pushing itself to the surface. "That is how he
was raised," Bözsi said, too self-absorbed to remark on
Anna's silence.

"When you saw him with his parents, it was hard to
believe these were people remotely related to the rest of us.
They seemed to breathe a different air than we did." She
smiled as she rewound some mental film, stashed away years
ago. "The old man, your grandfather, with his eternal bow
tie, mustache as stiff as a brush. Anyway . . ." she shrugged,
"after a while it didn't matter very much what they looked
like. Or anybody's personal theories on the subject of bloodlines, or the vintage of your baptismal papers and so on . . .
none of this mattered in the end. I'm famished," she said,
and reached for a piece of thickly crusted brown bread.
"The decor beats the service here, doesn't it?"

"Here he comes now," Anna said, grateful for the
waiter's distraction. The aggressively cheerful room had
become a kaleidoscope of displaced eyes and noses. Above
all Anna did not want Bözsi to know her own ignorance on
the topic of "bloodlines, baptismal papers, and so on . . ."

"When did you and my father become friends?" she
asked as they waited for their steaming bowls of goulash
soup to cool. Really, it was preposterous, the notion of this
overripe woman and her dry, eternally composed father,
friends. "Oh, we were always friends. I mean playmates,
from this high up," she indicated about one foot off the floor.
"We lived on the same street, you see. I suppose he has never
mentioned this? No, of course he wouldn't." She sighed.
"Not that it matters. This was such a long time ago. You
see, after the Nazis marched in . . . let's see, that was in the

spring . . . 1944, long before you were born! So maybe this
is a boring subject for you, this ancient history?"

"Not at all." Anna willed her voice to stay neutral. "In
fact," she said, reaching into her bag for a small black tape
recorder, "if you don't mind, I would like to record this. I
will need the background for the long piece I want to do
about the Hungarian Holocaust."

Bözsi eyed the machine suspiciously. "Zoli asked me to
be helpful," she said hesitantly. Anna doubted Bözsi was the
sort of woman who would do anything from a sense of
obligation. If Bözsi opened up to her childhood friend's
daughter, it would be entirely for her own reasons.

Anna pushed down the red record button, held her
breath, and waited. The tape wound by, made a scraping
sound, as it uselessly recorded the sound of Bözsi's spoon
clinking against the side of her soup bowl and the slurping
of her appreciative mouth.

"His mistake," Bözsi began after a while, "was he never
took me seriously. Because I liked to have a little fun. And
because I don't mind being who I am. I think maybe his
daughter will not make the same mistake?" She pushed another piece of bread into her mouth.

It was raining and dark by the time they left the restaurant, the darkness of late afternoon. Anna was glad of the
rain, for it abbreviated the parting rituals. She could grasp
Bözsi's hand warmly, thank her, and urge her to an impatient taxi, all under cover of the rain and darkness.

Twenty

I HAD FORGOTTEN how beautiful the city is," Anna's postcard read. "I've been up to the old house already . . . chilling how unchanged it all seems. And apart from a few new folds, so does Zoli! I've also met a childhood friend of yours: Erzsébet Miklos. 'Bözsi,' who, I suspect, has changed quite a bit since you last saw her. . . ."

Alex hadn't thought about any of them for so long. Now it was all rushing back. So she had already found Zoli. Bözsi. And by now maybe Laci. He could think of nothing else. It was his present life that increasingly struck him as paperthin, temporary.

He had returned to Budapest after two years in Barcelona puffed up with useless outrage and conviction. Of what use were either of those fine qualities in his situation? For by then things were beginning to slip away from Alex. All the known and trusted props of his life were sliding slowly out from under him. Things began to change, or so it seemed, the day his father removed from his buttonhole the tiny rosette, an award for valor in the Great War. A recent edict excluded war heroes possessed of Jewish blood from that elite.

The Bator's house on the Hill of Roses oppressed him like a shroud now. It felt absurdly large and much too cloistered from the world he had glimpsed. He could see his mother and father gradually retreat from a reality they found more and more frightening. His father, a diminutive and upright man, walked on legs rigid with arthritis. His face, though, was as pink and unlined as a baby's. The elder Bator now stopped his daily visit to his club. Instead, he passed the time sitting in front of a cracked, dark, Renaissance *Madonna*. "The work of an artist of the da Vinci School," he never tired of pointing out. What comfort, his son wondered, did this sweet, vague man draw from the somber recesses of the rock formation behind the *Madonna?*

Two or three times a day, his father consulted his wall barometer, rapped twice on its glass cover, and looked off into his private landscape. "You know, Klara," he said to his wife during one of their endless lunches, still served by Mariska (who claimed she was too old to worry about the law forbidding a Christian from serving in a Jewish household). "Maybe I was wrong. Maybe I should have had myself baptized, when you did." He shrugged. "We have always been Jews. It never seemed to matter much before." Alex wished he were still in Barcelona. Memories of the dead and the dying were less excrutiating than listening to this conversation between his parents.

"It never mattered before," he heard his mother say, "because we never called attention to ourselves. We were like the rest. Now, they have an excuse to despise us. It has become the proper way to behave. But, Sandor," she lowered her voice. "It was *there* all along."

And his mother smoothed her large skirt and absently touched the faded cameo that was a fixture at her throat. "You certainly thought me ridiculous at the time." She recalled her own "conversion" at sixteen or seventeen. One afternoon, she slipped into the dark of St. Matthew's Cathedral by the back door. A catechism and a large roll of forints bulged in her pocket. Five minutes later, her forehead still moist from the holy water with which the old priest had sprinkled her, she was a member of the Roman Catholic Church.

"I've told Mariska not to bother about fish on Fridays anymore," she said to her husband. "The archbishop seems to have forgotten us completely." Klara Bator sighed. (Alex remembered the many summer weekends he and his parents had spent in the company of that wry Franciscan. The archbishop's farm was surrounded by cherry orchards in the hills above the Danube. As adolescents, the archbishop and Alex's mother had carried on a brief but much discussed flirtation.) "This used to be such a civilized place." His mother sighed again.

What was the point of planning exile to any other of the Bator's preferred corners of the map? Those places where in the past you could count on good coffee, real linen, and polite company in any season. They, too, had stopped being "civilized."

At Budapest University, where Alex was Assistant Professor of Classics, he was now told he could never aspire to a full professorship. "Sub Pondere Crescit Palma," the owlish little man who was head of the department told Alex, one frail hand touching his shoulder. The Palm Grows

Under Pressure. Possibly the aphorism made some sense in the Rome of Tacitus, Alex thought.

He began to spend more and more time at the university's Athletic Club. Sophocles and Plato no longer fired his imagination. Instead, he worked out with his foils until every sinew and ligament in his arms and legs protested.

In that Spartan, dimly lit training room, with its musty smell of sweat and leather, until now only skill had counted. The members had been preoccupied by other things than helpful homilies or pointed questions. Once they pronounced you worthy; only the lightness of your movements and the speed of your foils had mattered. The club was peopled by the sons of the country's titled and expensive names.

None of his fellows on the fencing team yet suspected Alex Bator's true origins. They were all, however, aware of Nathan Goldman's. Goldman was beginning to stalk the gymnasium with the air of panic of a man nobody wants on his team anymore.

Alex was making quick thrusts into a leather practice bag when he heard the unmistakable, insinuating voice of Tamás Losoncy. "Come on, Nate," said the tall, pale Losoncy, wearing nothing but his white knickerbockers. Perspiration from his morning workout trickled down his smooth, well-muscled chest. He had removed the rubber tip from his epée. "It'll be more fun without the gear. You need the practice anyway." His face was slashed by a smile that made Alex's skin turn hot and prickly. "Haven't had much action lately," Losoncy's epée began to pry Goldman's mask off his face, "have you?"

Goldman's eyes were stretched wide with fear. Alex

could see him paralyzed by terror, unable to move or speak. Fencing, for Goldman, was a polite diversion he performed for his parents' sake. They had a well-known compulsion for the essential trappings of gentility. Under no circumstances would he ever voluntarily offer himself as a match for Tamás Losoncy, the university's star fencer. Alex suspected it was the first time Losoncy had ever even looked at Goldman.

Suddenly, Alex couldn't just stand there and watch. He whipped off his own mask. A thick curtain of sweat blurred his vision. Anger, like an obstruction in his throat, choked him. Without thinking, he strode up to the grinning, perspiring man. "I'll fence with you, Losoncy."

"Hey, what's it to you, Bator?" Losoncy asked with a sneer. "Not another Jew, are you?"

With one movement, Alex yanked off his fencing glove and with his bare palm slapped the man with all his strength. Losoncy lurched to one side. His cheek turned a blotchy red and he had stopped smiling. Rubbing the sting from his palm, Alex turned on his heel and walked away from his stunned teammates and out of the club.

The slap had caught him as off-guard as its grotesque target. But he didn't want to analyze his motives because he hated introspection, feared what it would churn up. Of course, he knew: he loathed being thought of as a Jew. He did not think of himself as one. If anything, he identified more with the dry nonchalance of Tamás Losoncy than with the exposed, terrified Nathan Goldman. That was how he had been raised: impatient with the unassimilated Jews of his country, contemptuous of the likes of Goldman.

The Bators were European to their fingertips. They regarded the Renaissance as their finest hour and thought of

Beethoven and Wagner as *their* composers. Berlin was their Athens. And Jews were, for the most part, sadly lacking in breeding and subtlety. And always, well, Jewish.

Alex remembered the old Jewish District of Pest. When he walked through it, it was always very quickly. The gutteral speech and the pungent smells that floated from every window struck him as disturbingly exotic. Even more foreign, he thought, than the lifestyle of the Moroccan Berbers he had photographed on a recent vacation. No, Mount Zion would never be his Mecca.

By the early forties, Alex's Christian friends (for Zoli and Bözsi were his sole Jewish connections) suddenly appeared to have more obligations than before. Others paused for an imperceptible beat before reaching for his hand or rising to greet him. He began to avoid his friends. One by one, he pruned away the routine social encounters of his former life. He would not give anyone the opportunity to diminish his dignity. Better to do your own diminishing.

Twenty-one

STRETCHED OUT ON her bed, queasy from the wine with which she had kept Bözsi's words flowing, Anna pushed down the black replay button on her tape recorder. This familiar motion, playing back the background material that generally preceded her actual taped interview, jolted her into a realization. She had not closed the preliminaries with Bözsi with her usual question. She had not asked in her familiar way, voice carefully modulated to mask impatience, "Would you be willing to say these things in front of a UNS camera?" In fact she was quite confident Bözsi, whose vanity was beyond restraint, would have replied, "Well, why not? What have I got to hide?"

For Bözsi would know that her flickering image on a screen would certainly be seen, hundreds of miles away, by a man who had once badly bruised her female pride. Bözsi now had the power to remind Alex of the very things he had gone to such pains to leave behind. But Anna had not asked this of Bözsi. For though she had come (or so she had told Abe Levin) in search of "a story," it had now been transformed into her own story. This was careless, unprofessional behavior, and Levin was not the sort of man, hers was not the sort of profession, that allowed a personal indulgence. Anna sensed she was headed for dangerous ground, for she lacked the will to stop this from happening. Worse, a part of her reached out for this danger. But just then all of her attention strained toward the breathless voice that seeped from her small black tape recorder:

"You see, he had been raised a gentleman . . . and then all at once that position was no longer open to him. The trouble was he wasn't prepared to try anything else. Which is why I think he eventually fell in with Laci. László Andor. You've heard of him maybe even in New York? A very big man these days. But this is jumping ahead of my story. . . .

"We never believed any of this would happen to us, you see. Oh, we had heard about the Jews in those other places, the Slovaks, the Ruthenians, the Czechs. The Dutch and the French even. But not us. We would survive. Hungary has always been an odd place, you see. I mean, a parliamentary state with its silly attachment to a mythical royal crown. A non-Slav land in a sea of Slavs—with this mysterious language of ours. So, again we would not follow our neighbors' example. Not that we didn't have our own typically charming version of anti-Semitism. Not at all the same crude variety the Germans, Austrians, and Poles favored, though. They used to say here that an anti-Semite was someone who hated the Jews even more than was necessary . . . so you see. . . ."

Bözsi said nobody in Hungary really took Hitler's ravings seriously. Not the majority Christian population, not the Jews. He was deemed Austrian low life and his hysterical outpourings only embarrassed people like the Bators. But meanwhile the government was quietly running up a big bill to the Führer. For Hitler had helped Hungary to dismember her neighbors, to retrieve territory Budapest had lost during World War I, when once again she found herself on the wrong side. And finally one million Jews sitting pretty in the heart of a Jew-free Reich became more than Hitler could swallow.

"So, very slowly, we Jews lost our last layer of protection: the Head of State, the well-bred anti-Semite in his gold-braided uniform, Regent Horthy, who sneered at Hitler's crude methods for dealing with the 'Jewish Problem.' But Horthy soon ran out of excuses to give Berlin. 'I've taken their jobs away, their position in society . . . even their radios! What more do you expect me to do?' the old boy asked Hitler. Of course Hitler had plenty of ideas. But by 1944 he didn't think Horthy was up to the job. And you see the Hungarian Nazi Party on its own didn't amount to much. A bunch of down-and-out thugs, the Arrow Cross. So Berlin decided to send in the specialists.

"It was in early spring—when Eichmann and his Einsatzcommando rolled in and set up their headquarters atop one of Buda's pretty hills.

"Eichmann . . . God, I saw him once," Bözsi breathed a deep, raspy breath, "a face you never forget, the face itself was a broken promise . . . And yet so many believed him! Because they needed to. My father did. He was one of eight men Eichmann summoned to form the Jewish Council. That was the first thing he did. Eichmann needed their help to keep the rest of us from going wild. Eight frightened old men: bankers, lawyers, industrialists (my father owned a big

light bulb concern). I remember he called home from the
lobby of the Majestic Hotel after that first session, and he
whispered into the phone, 'It's going to be all right. They
only want us to cooperate.' My God, cooperate!

"The next day they got their first list of demands: six
hundred mattresses and the evacuation within fifteen minutes of all Jewish buildings, schools, and places of worship.
Now all Gestapo property. But everything was done according to schedule. 'He's not such a bad sort,' my father
kept telling us. 'He has his job. We have ours.'

"Well, part of Eichmann's job was to reduce us from
human beings into his little pet mice . . . each day a little
more. First you couldn't ride the trolley. Then theaters and
movies and swimming pools were off limits. Then you
couldn't even sit on a park bench. But the Jewish Council
kept saying, 'Wear the star! It will protect you!' Well, I *did*
wear the star. Which made your father furious because he
of course never did. He told me, 'With your blue eyes, no
one would guess you were Jewish.' Finally he talked me into
getting baptized. But even then I could not please him. The
line of people waiting for certificates was so long in front of
the Catholic church, I walked over to the Greek Orthodox.
No waiting there. 'Only *you* would choose to convert to
Greek Orthodoxy,' Alex said afterwards.

"Around this time he was having his own problems, you
see . . . there was an incident that made quite a stir. Alex
slapped some high-born hooligan in his club. I will never
forget one of the last lunches I had at the Bators' house. You
see, his mother was very fond of me. I think I was the only
person who ever made her laugh. I mean really laugh. Out
loud. Such a difficult lady . . . so even though Alex had no

time for me anymore, I was often around . . . And from childhood habit he confided in me still. And because he was very lonely now. I knew this, that in a way he was using me, to keep the isolation from choking him. I didn't mind."

Twenty-two

ONE WEEK AFTER he slapped Losoncy, Alex received the university's quaintly worded dismissal letter. It was in the scorching heat of mid-August. Alex had been preparing his opening lecture for the fall semester.

His voice was dead calm when he announced during lunch, 'I've resigned my post at the university. Five years of teaching dimwits and ruffians is enough for anyone. Besides," he shrugged, and reached into his pocket for one of his English cigarettes, "these days, they could care less about Plato. Who can blame them?"

"What will you do?" his father asked in a frail voice.

"I'll find something." He smiled. "Don't worry, Papa. I never thought of myself as a teacher. That was only temporary."

"Why is this soup so greasy?" his mother asked with a frown. "Mariska doesn't seem to have her heart in it anymore." And the subject of the university never came up again. His mother, at least, understood that the last connection to their former world had been severed.

It was several months after this that László Andor called him. Alex was surprised at the pleasure the man's voice gave him. "What have you been up to?" he asked. They had neither seen each other nor spoken since Spain. Spain! His grand, youthful adventure, a century before. Laci was a reminder of this other life.

"Oh, more of the same," Laci replied in his monosyllabic way. "I need to talk to you, Alex. There's a roadside tavern in Ujpest, just outside the electronics works. Four o'clock is good for me. Before the factory whistle blows."

Laci didn't ask if the time suited Bator. Alex assumed his former comrade had heard he had been fired by the university.

Alex did not tell his parents he was going to a café whose stench would make their stomachs turn, to meet a man his mother would not have trusted to drive her car. His anger, like some ripe fruit nourished by daily humiliation, was ready to burst. That much he knew. Beyond that, he really had no plans.

He could still eat and sleep and move around town, but he was no longer able to ride the tram. Alex's dignity was ragged over a wound he suspected would never heal. Nor did he have the consolation of any other community. He didn't want that! He had looked down on "them" all his life. So why were they thrust upon him now? He had nothing to do with Jews. An accident of birth. He preferred the self-destruction Laci was offering.

Laci was slumped in the smoke-filled corner of a café that smelled sour from cheap wine and deprivation. His hands were stuffed inside his frayed trousers and a check-ered cap all but covered his face. Laci looked up and saw his friend recoil. "What on earth has happened to you?" Alex asked. Laci's bones looked sharp under loose skin. He smiled and showed more gums than teeth.

"In and out of the arms of the Special Branch." Laci grinned. "Picayune stuff. Handing out leaflets, throwing them over factory walls. For that you get a sponge in your mouth so the gentle population isn't annoyed by the sound of screams when they hold a cigarette to certain of my favorite possessions. To get the comrades' names."

They looked at each other without speaking. Neither man had much faith in words. In Spain, each had observed the other, and knew what he was capable of. Besides, neither the Jew nor the Communist had all that many options.

"And yourself? Not so good. Huh?" Laci did not wait for an answer. "I've got an offer to make you, Alex. From the higher-ups." He paused, waited for the other man to react. Alex was still.

"You've got the brains and the background for something big," Laci began. Yes, this was also what Alex had assumed. A man of his breeding, his ability to drop the right passwords to open the right doors was surely meant for something big. Immune to danger. But he realized all the Bator ancestors, those landowners, the merchants and the polished scoundrels, they were had! They had paid their dues to a feudal society, and believed their sons and grandsons would inherit the benefits of their fealty. Their world was finished.

"What do you want me to do?" he heard himself ask, knowing a part of him still regarded Laci's creed as a dark and unpredictable force. But the Nazis, in their drive to forge a European Übermensch, had taken Alex's own ideals of order and cultural superiority, pulled them out of shape, and claimed them as their own. Alex's only escape hatches were in moral and intellectual death. What did it matter? They probably wouldn't survive anyway.

"Something suited to your gifts." Laci's swollen eyes swept Alex's sartorial splendor. Even in those days, Alex continued to dress as though he had someplace to go. It had been some time since he had bought any new clothes. But he still wore a vest under his soft tweed jacket and his necktie still perched atop a gold collar pin.

"We want you to make yourself available to the Western press," Laci said, lowering his voice to a whisper. "You need the work. They need someone in Budapest. You've got all the skills. The manners, the language. After all those words you've spilled on Plato, this should be kid stuff." Laci searched his friend's face for a reaction, but found none.

"Call this number." Laci pushed a smudged wrinkled piece of notepaper across the greasy table. "Jeremy McDonald," it read. *The Daily Telegraph.* Geneva, Switzerland." It sounded like a different planet.

"We know this outfit is looking for somebody here to report on the final fireworks. Call them. And sell yourself. And, Alex," Laci leaned so close, Alex held his own breath. "Don't think of yourself as one of us. Just a question of mutual needs," he said with a toothless smile. Then he reached inside his threadbare jacket and produced an envelope which he dropped in front of Alex. "Your round-trip airfare to Geneva, and the papers to get you out of the country. Pretty professional job, huh? Not that they'll give you much trouble at the airport. You're not exactly a flaming advertisement for your sect. Blew my mind when

I found out, to tell you the truth," he said, his lower lip twisted in a smile.

Alex picked up the envelope and the bit of paper. He had just about exhausted his savings. On this, too, the Party was well informed. He needed the trip and he needed the job. Above all, he needed to be needed. The future did not exist for him anyway. Getting through the present was sufficient challenge. Danger was better than humiliation, wasn't it? Anything was.

Laci got up from the table. "I'll call you when you're working for the *Daily Telegraph.*" He shambled away. Alex watched him fade quickly into the dismal landscape of factory towers and gray working-class blocks.

Twenty-three

ALEX'S HEAD was throbbing by the time his noisy prop plane landed at Geneva Airport. His legs still felt watery under him as he walked along the quai looking for the Beau Rivage Restaurant. The eerie tranquility of the place. There were no uniforms, no air raids, no sirens; just a polite, disorienting normality. People strolled, shopped, and lunched as though the world had not yet lost its head.

"Mr. Bator, is it? How do you do?" The hand that reached for Alex's was long, pale, and noncommittally limp in his own.

Jeremy McDonald was the sort of breezy Englishman Alex might have enjoyed in a different situation. Under the circumstances, McDonald's dispassion and his elaborate courtesy were about as soothing for Alex's nerves as the sound of a nail scraping a wall. "I've ordered an old bottle of Something-or-Other-'24—a decent vintage, they said—to toast what I trust will be a pleasant association," he said, raising his glass and one eyebrow.

Alex tried to match him for each name and place he dropped, his heart no longer in the old game. McDonald asked very few hard questions. They agreed the Nazis were boors and their leader a dangerous (and, equally damning, humorless) lunatic. But for the Englishman, the whole subject was less compelling than who had the best shot at the Derby that year.

They ate oysters for lunch. In Budapest, the Bators dipped stale bread in hot fat for dinner. Alex sat across a pink damask tablecloth from an English gentleman who spoke of Hitler and the Ballets Russes in the same breath. "Start off with a few lifestyle pieces on the Jews," McDonald suggested. "All these rumors flying about. Look into how much is fact, how much invention." Alex promised he would check out the rumors.

After lunch, they strolled along the lake, past the luxury hotels. McDonald patted Alex's shoulder. "Keep us posted on the Boches's next move, won't you? And do look after yourself. No extra fee for getting in trouble, old boy."

Alex would have given his right arm to stay on in Geneva. Budapest seemed light-years away from all that Swiss boredom and decency. But he would never abandon his parents.

That evening he tuned in to the BBC's World Service. "Lieutenant Colonel Adolf Eichmann," the clipped Oxford accent cut through the crackle, "has been dispatched by the Führer to oversee the solution to 'the problem' of Europe's final surviving Jewish community. The Nazi officer has already set up his headquarters in a residential hotel in Budapest." Unlike McDonald, the BBC no longer regarded "Judenfrei Europa" as unconfirmed rumor.

Alex filled his lungs with the crisp, clean air of Lake Geneva. His face set in the grim resignation of the condemned, he boarded the plane back to Budapest.

Twenty-four

He never had a chance to let McDonald know what "the Boches's next move" was. Alex himself was engulfed by that move. It was spring, and there was a lush promise to that March of 1944 which struck many as a cruel jest of nature. The soft ripeness in the air, the feeling of life stirring beneath the surface, was in such brazen contrast to the events of the day. Alex and Bözsi stood on a street corner and watched the Wehrmacht pour into their deluded city.

Suddenly, mysteriously, every tree in Budapest had a slogan tacked to it: "*Now the Jews Will Get What's Coming to Them!*" There was a complete unreality to what was happening because nothing was reported in the newspapers and the radio played only the most soothing pieces of Wagner and Beethoven. Not a single official word regarding Hungary's new status as an occupied state was pronounced. People lived off the wildest rumors, which were never as wild as reality turned out to be.

Thanks to Sandor Bator's order of merit, the Bators were temporarily exempted from wearing the yellow star or from moving into a designated house. One afternoon Alex found his father in his customary place in front of his *Madonna*, a yarmulke on his balding head. Alex was stunned. There was no point in asking his father why, after a lifetime of scorning Jews, with the SS flooding the streets . . .

"He is like a baby, Alex," his mother whispered to her son. "You cannot treat him like an adult anymore."

Bözsi learned from her own father that lists were being prepared. The more prominent Jews would be the first to be rounded up. "I told Alex he should *do* something. Go into hiding, find a Christian friend, check into a hospital. Anything. But there was this lethargy about him. I just wanted to shake him. Tell him he would be no more immune than the rest of us. I think until the very last moment he felt he would be spared from the usual treatment. I tried talking sense into your grandfather but this was no longer possible. He would say, 'Doesn't Regent Horthy still play bridge with Leo Goldberger, the textile king, every Thursday?' and mumble these old Latin sayings like Extra Hungariam Non Est Vita . . . You know, outside Hungary there is no life. He was lost to us."

And then, one cold, bright, star-filled night just after Alex had finished listening to the BBC, the bell at the garden gate in the Bators' Budapest house slashed through the stillness. Alex was already in his pajamas. He leaned out of the window of his little house which was at the edge of his parents' property. It was as black out there as if the end of the world had already arrived. "Sicherheitsdienst!" a disembodied voice shouted. The SS.

There were two of them, a tall one and a short one. He greeted them in German. They were as polite as he was. He averted his eyes from the double lightning insignia on their collars and the death's-head badges on the visored hats they dropped on his desk. "Would you care for something to drink?" he asked, still a host, not yet a captive.

Why he had believed good behavior or poise made a difference in that situation, Bözsi couldn't explain. Shock perhaps had something to do with it. Nor did he have the habit of hysteria. Of course emotions he kept under suspicious guard, even from himself.

Alex was told to pack a small bag. They helped themselves to his brandy while he went upstairs to get ready. He saw that the light was still on in his parents' bedroom. But he could think of no way to alert them. What good would it do anyway? They did not ask to see his papers, but since they called him by his name, he assumed they were intimately familiar with his bloodlines. There was no mention then, or later, of his meeting in the seedy factory café with a renegade Communist. How he envied Laci Andor, bruised, toothless. Old before his time, but free!

He did not show them his baptismal certificate. He did not wish to give them the satisfaction of telling him any Jew with $50 could get his hands on one.

Moments later Alex Bator was riding in the back of a small Mercedes with the license plate POL. The city was dark and peaceful. Bator was no longer any part of it.

The Eastern Railway Station was an anthill of activity. Hundreds of men with the vacant look of sleepwalkers thronged the platform. Some of them had rucksacks on their backs, as if off on a Sunday hike. Suddenly, they were encircled. The Gendarmerie, wearing riding breeches and the cock-feathered kepis that had come to symbolize terror, closed in on the dazed humanity. Alex was among the first in the train.

He swore then that if he survived, he would not talk about any of this, to anyone. Mourning and remembrance were two more self-indulgences he would eliminate.

Alex was in a train marked "Useful Jews": fodder for the Forced Labor Brigade. Not that this privilege altered his travel conditions. He was shoved into a cattle car without enough space to lie down, without food, water, or a latrine for a two-day journey. The stench was what he remembered afterwards. The odor of urine, then later, vomit.

The train twisted its way through thatched-roof villages of low, whitewashed stucco huts. Alex could make out cows pulling cartloads of hay and, in the distance, horses dragging plows across muddy fields, as they had for centuries. The dark shapes of peasant women in their traditional black headscarves passed almost close enough to touch his freight train. He kept shifting his position: he stood up, crouched, slumped his head between his knees. His long body ached unbearably.

At one point the entire train screeched to a halt somewhere in open country. Alex peered through the cracks. He saw a large van, like a furniture moving truck, pull up not far from the car directly behind his own. Gendarms formed a sort of honor guard between the train and the van. Slowly, the passengers began to file in front of the smartly uniformed Guardsmen. Two by two they boarded the van. They were old and bent, and Alex could hear them mumbling the same prayers he had heard repeated by his fellow passengers.

When he saw them shut the door, he understood. It was

the sort of door he had only seen on bank vaults before. The truck's engine began to roar. A few minutes later, he and the others began to cough and wheeze. Gas from the van's exhaust filled their nostrils, burned their eyes, and made their skin crawl under its accumulated sweat and dirt. About five minutes passed and then nothing. Silence. The rest of the mixed transport, relieved now of its cargo of Useless Jews, chugged its way to the Eastern Front.

Twenty-five

Hey, professor," the guard barked one day. "Get your stuff together and get over here." After six weeks of trench digging near the Rumanian border, Alex had mastered the forced labor camp routine. He had even made a friend. Gyula Neumann's subtle appreciation of the classics helped while away the long nights out in the open.

"You're gonna make a little trip," the guard informed him now. Alex assumed any change would have to be for the worse. "God bless you," he heard Gyula shout after him as he climbed aboard the waiting truck, ice cold, but composed.

"Kistarcsa," Bözsi cleared her throat and long seconds of silence reeled by on the tape, "one of those names dragged down by the most unforgiving ghosts . . . That was his next stop. From the front to a little village just north of Budapest. A serene setting of green fields dotted by people milling in seeming disarray. And the inmates weren't caked in mud. There were women as well as men. Animals grazed peacefully. And Budapest only half an hour away! It was a camp, of course, but a humane one, which allowed us inmates the sweet possibility of hope. This is where I saw your father for the last time."

In Kistarcsa, Alex also found his parents. His once debonair father no longer stood very straight, nor was he particularly clean. Sandor shuffled about the dusty courtyard, eyes hazy with an unformed question. He still did not use a stick, but now leaned on his wife for support. Someone had removed the yarmulke from the old man's head.

During his last days of freedom he had wrapped up his *Madonna,* his final sustenance, and carried it to SS headquarters. He presented the portrait to an Oberführer Geschke, who had a reputation as a lover of art. This was how he hoped to buy his son's freedom. "So," the SS lieutenant had asked him with an ingratiating smile, "you collect the icons of different faiths? And your rabbi does not object?" The old man had no answer. He looked at his *Madonna* a final time and invited the officer to keep it, in exchange for his son. That was how the Bators all ended up in the relative tranquility of Kistarcsa.

Alex tried to avoid looking at the six-pointed yellow star that covered the spot left by Sandor Bator's order of merit.

Klara Bator seemed strangely rejuvenated. Though a cotton kerchief all but covered her gray hair, she held her head high. The soft white hands that used to lie limp in her lap, in anticipation of some vague affliction, now covered her husband's gnarled and spotted fingers. Klara's thin, bluish lips were pursed tight in determination. She had made a decision to survive.

The old lady wept softly at the sight of her son. Alex's cheeks were sucked in, lifeless, his complexion sallow from a diet of potatoes and watery soup. Dirt filled the deep creases that slashed his forehead and cheeks. "Oh, but alive!" she sniffed. "You're alive, my boy."

"Alex didn't seem surprised to see me there," Bözsi said. " 'Is this where the Greek Orthodox shelter their flock?' he asked in that mocking tone he had always used with me. But there wasn't any weight left to it . . . his superior air. He looked like a man who'd been punched so hard in the stomach he has no wind left."

Then one day, a word started making the camp rounds. At first it was whispered, shrugged off, silenced like an obscenity. Then it came back to stay: Deportation. It spread like an infection. Lists, it was said, were again being drawn up. The trains were on the way. And one day after lunch, they lined everybody up. Age or health or sex made no difference. Whether you were one half or one quarter Jewish did not matter either. Somebody wanted Kistarcsa closed down. Baptismal certificates were crumpled by mildly amused guards.

Planted in the camp courtyard under a blazing midsummer sun, Bözsi, the Bators, and their fellow inmates clutched their meager belongings, while guards barked out fifteen hundred names. Six hours later, night was falling and a long line of trucks had pulled up to take them to the trains. "I can still hear the sound of moans and prayers buzzing in my ear. I saw them carry the sick and the old to the trains and still vaguely hoped I was dreaming. The thud of rifle butts against soft flesh and whimpers that sounded more animal than human . . . they were no dream. I kept one eye out for Alex all the time, but I don't think he noticed me . . . or anything else for that matter.

"The doors slammed shut behind us. The gendarms bolted them from outside. That is a terrible, an unforgettable sound . . ." Bözsi fell momentarily silent. "The train began to pick up speed. A few moments later, our ears were split by the screech of the locomotive. Our clumsy cargo of ten cars ground to a jerky halt. They'd decided to save on transport and finish us off in the middle of open country. We decided that was it for sure.

"But again we heard the locomotive building steam. The hissing and puffing was coming so close. And then our own car came alive again, moving at first very hesitantly, and then pumping hard and heading not west toward the Germans and what we most feared, but in the opposite direction! A new locomotive had been attached to the rear of the train and was pulling us all back toward Budapest. Back to Kistarcsa.

"Can you imagine the delirium inside the train? Our faces, sagging with despair a moment before, lifted by hesitant smiles. We embraced strangers and wept the tears of people returned from their own deaths. I saw Alex cradling his mother in his arms. I think that was the last time I ever saw them . . . any of them.

"Kistarcsa seemed like Paradise now. Before long we found out who was responsible for this act of divine intervention. Adolf Eichmann, the man who was only doing his job, had ordered the camp shut and all internees dispatched to Auschwitz. But the Nazi lieutenant colonel failed to inform Regent Horthy, still the nominal chief of state, of his move. When word reached Horthy that a trainload of 'his' Jews was on its way to the death camp, the old Admiral exploded in rage and injured pride. He ordered the train stopped and returned to Kistarcsa. Horthy would teach Eichmann who was in charge! Fifteen hundred of us were alive as a result of a chess game that was not yet over.

"Soon after this incident I managed to 'liberate' myself from Kistarcsa. A guard, a big-boned boy with the crooked teeth of a country bumpkin, took thirty seconds to fall in love. I paid dearly for this freedom, believe me." Bözsi laughed her low laugh. "I heard Alex got out, too. The old people, I don't know. We were so busy trying to survive . . . I never found out what became of them. I do know that very few of us got out of Kistarcsa alive. I think about those people . . . more often than I would like. Maybe Alex does, too?"

Twenty-six

ANNA DID NOT KNOW much about what it meant to be a Jew. She had a vague notion it had to do with anguish and introspection, straining for some sort of truth. A rich life of the spirit. In short, the things she had done without. The things *he* had chosen to withhold from her, as a trade-off for what she was: cosmopolitan, poised, and safe. Offending no one. Standing for nothing.

Had she ever confronted him with the question, "Are you Jewish?" no doubt her father would have said, quietly, sadly, "Yes. We are of Jewish origin." Surely an outright lie was beyond him.

He had lived a lie for her. He had made her believe he had nothing to do with those outcasts and their eternal wanderings and hopeless struggles in a world that, given half a chance, would turn on them yet again. He had sculpted himself into the embodiment of everything Anna thought Jews were not: aloof and indifferent to the past and to any God. The perfect cover. And she, his child, had been raised to fulfill his idea of perfection.

How simple and emotionally satisfying it would have been to feel only compassion for what he had been through. But her compassion was diluted by other, harder emotions. She felt duped. She had not penetrated something that was hers by right.

She recalled now her parents' alarm when she returned after two years at the London School of Economics accompanied by a tall, fair-haired Israeli sabra. Before long, her parents succeeded in making the boy seem too clumsy in her eyes to be regarded as a serious suitor. They turned qualities that in London she had found irresistible, a raw liveliness he radiated, his unabashed sensuality, into embarrassing handicaps. Anna sent him home after two weeks, puzzled by her own rapid change of heart. But in those days she regarded her parents as more worldly and knowing than anyone else she knew. Surely their experience and judgment exceeded hers.

This must be like finding out at age thirty-six that your parents aren't your real parents, she thought. Was the feverish Roman Catholicism of her childhood one more layer of protection they had applied, like an ointment? Then it hit her like a thunderclap: she had never actually seen her father in church! Not once in all the years when she had been convinced she would be struck down by divine wrath if she were not in her pew on Sunday morning, did he ever accompany her past the front door of the humble little neighborhood church of her childhood. How was it she had never made anything of that? She felt embarrassed now and foolish.

She was grateful for one thing. Her own views on the subject were uncomplicated. The militant Catholicism of

her childhood paled in the New World. She found the
suburban cinderblock and linoleum churches, their endless
pot-luck suppers and Christmas bazaars, bland and unneces-
sary in her new life. She soon stopped attending Mass.

As a result of her American upbringing, she regarded
Jews as probably brighter and more enterprising than the
rest. And more musical. She loved music, and had always
attributed part of the genius of the Sterns, the Perlmans, and
Menuhins to some mysterious aspect of their Jewishness.
What Jews did in the privacy of their own homes, away
from their paler, less exotic friends, she knew nothing about.
She knew it took courage to be one. She had grown up
thinking her father was the bravest man in the world.

"I knew Alex would marry a Christian," Bözsi had told
her. "He was such a snob, you know." So her mother's
Christianity at least was genuine. Her mother with all her
familiar vanities and everyday frailties, the keeper of this
immense secret. Anna had always felt a residual, childish
resentment of her. She felt her mother had once deliberately
chosen Alex over Anna. For Julia need not have worked so
closely alongside Alex and thus covered herself with sufficient incriminating evidence in the eyes of the State to land
in jail. Anna was also often impatient with Julia's simpering
submission to her husband's every mood. There was no fight
left in Julia, no anger or temper, just long looks of muffled
suffering.

What made this doubly hard for Anna to accept was that
she knew her mother had not always been this way. There
were still reminders of another Julia. Pictures of a woman
with mocking green eyes, slender and full of barely con-

tained pleasure in life. It wasn't fair, Anna had often thought petulantly, that I never really knew this woman. For Julia, like some exotic flower that cannot be transplanted, seemed to droop and fade with each year in the United States. And occasionally her parents would exchange a look, a word, between themselves which locked Anna out completely and let her know there was a whole life she had missed out on. Now she knew what those coded looks were about.

Together, however, her parents had raised her free from the mark of hate her father had lived under. Only now she could see that her mother had extracted a price for Anna's ignorance. Julia had cast a shadow over moments that should have been simple and bright.

In her later years, Julia was often unwell, and her ailments seemed aggravated in direct proportion to Anna's well-being. Julia had fainted while Anna delivered her high school valedictory speech. Her mother's pallor and the image of her limp body being lifted to a couch were Anna's sole surviving memories of that occasion. And again during Sarah's birth, Julia's pains came almost simultaneously with the onset of Anna's labor. Alex and Sam's attention thus shifted abruptly to Julia. Anna spent her time in the hospital making anxious phone calls inquiring about her mother's health, while Sarah squealed in the crib next to her bed.

In the end it was Julia's voice that gave her away. Fear had been permanently lodged in that voice, the way a shard from a bullet can merge into an organism. "Hello," she would answer the telephone in anxious tremolo, like a sentry firing a warning shot into nowhere. "Don't come a step closer," it seemed to say, the most frail yet guarded voice

Anna had ever heard. "I have you covered," it seemed to whisper.

The clues had been there all along. But the pieces were just beginning to drop into place. Anna had never really known her parents.

Twenty-seven

Hᴇ ᴅɪᴅɴ'ᴛ ʜᴀᴠᴇ ᴛᴏ ꜱᴀʏ or do much," Anna
mused. "There was a dignity about him . . . and a hurt I
couldn't understand. For a long time his presence was
enough." Anna and Christopher sat side by side on his
couch, her legs tucked under her, his feet propped up by a
glass coffee table. "I remember drifting off to the clickety-
clack of his typewriter, the sound of Beethoven's Violin
Concerto in the background. Their combined sound was the
most beautiful symphony I could imagine.

"This isn't only the usual Freudian father-daughter obsession," she said defensively. "Zoli seems to have been just
as entranced by him . . . even as a child. But the truth is, the
deeper I probe, the more blurred his image becomes." She
stood up and impatiently smoothed an imaginary wrinkle
from her skirt. "One thing I can't do," she said, as if answering his unspoken question, "is pull back and let it go now,
Christopher. I've gone too far. Anyway," she said briskly,
"I've opened the channel for you, haven't I? Dear old Uncle
Zoli . . ."

Shepherd smiled. He listened to her like an anthropologist, as though he had heard other tales, similar to hers, in other corners of the globe. Nothing surprised him. Somehow he seemed to know more, understand more about Anna than she herself. At a time when so many of her foundations were shifting under her, he had become her anchor. She was drawn to the calm of his knowing, slightly ironic features. She used her hotel room mostly to make her by now pro forma phone calls to spur Comrade Fekete into action. Most nights she was at Shepherd's place.

"It's amazing how many things you can do with eggs," she said, emerging after a while from his little-used cubbyhole of a kitchen with a frying pan that smelled deliciously of tomatoes, onions, and green peppers. "I owe my omelette-making genius to the London School of Economics. I couldn't even afford the curry carry-outs in Kensington, so I developed this unmatched repertoire for survival." He poured them each a glass of ruby-red Egri Bikavér, Bull's Blood wine. *"Egészségedre,"* he said, raising his glass to her.

She smiled. "You just told me to do something terrible to myself. The accent is on the *third* syllable. If you're toasting my health, that is."

"Your health and a few others things," he said returning her smile, and pushing back his chair.

"You know," she said, looking around his sparsely furnished place, "this is my only home in Budapest now."

"Really? I've never thought of it as home. Just a room with a view," he said, lightly patting her offered hand.

"Where is home, then?" she asked softly.

"No such place." He shook his head and smiled.

"Well, it feels too strange for me to be staying in a hotel," she said, deliberately changing her tone to match his, "with my old house just minutes away. Though I'm not quite sure what's left to connect me to that place. Our apartment has been split in two. I hear a wall runs right through my old room." She looked away, fixed suddenly on the view, despising her own sentimentality and her too-sharp need of him. This domestic scene, and all it implied, was clearly making him uncomfortable.

"But your memories of that house aren't all that cheerful, are they?" he asked.

"That's not quite true," she answered irritably. "I mean, not entirely true. I first made up my mind to be famous and beautiful in that room. And to see New York," she said, in the tinny voice she normally saved for strangers and cocktail parties.

There was something about his face, however, the fine lines carved permanently into the skin that was almost transparent, which moved her deeply that instant. She wanted him to touch her, yet was afraid to speak. No youth could ever affect her this way, that she knew. She did not believe a young face could hold this range of possibilities. "Damn you," she whispered. "Do you know how . . . how . . . handsome you are?" There was a slight break in her voice. "Really. Beautiful."

"I might have been." He laughed. "Or so I was told."

"I don't believe that," she said. "I don't believe it was possible before now."

"Before you, you mean? You've transformed me from frog to prince?"

"I just don't believe you were born with that expression in your eyes. A look that switches between wanting me and not wanting me. Wanting to be happy and pushing it away. I think you had to earn that look."

But he seemed to have stopped hearing her words. Leaning close, he ran a finger along her forehead, down her nose
to her lips. His finger stayed on her lips, which stopped
moving. He kissed her softly. She did not move while he
opened her blouse and lightly touched her. He held her and
seemed momentarily lost in the smell of her, pressed her so
close her breathing came hard. "You are so fine," he
breathed. She put his hand on her breast so he would feel
the hard pounding beneath his touch.

He led her to his bed and covered her with his body.
They did not speak, but made love for a long time. She
understood it was much easier for him not to speak. Her
body seemed to trust his completely. She was aware that her
smart reporter's reflexes had been functioning at half power
when it came to him. The only place she really felt safe was
there, in Shepherd's arms. Until now this had been enough.

"Your clothes conceal too much," he said, looking at
her. "They cut you into little pieces." He smiled. "There is
a whole world here," he said, his hands running down her
hips across her belly.

She reached for the sheet that lay rumpled at the bottom
of the bed and covered them both. "You've asked me so few
questions," he said, easing her into the soft place beneath his
shoulder. "I assume others must have told you?"

"Yes," she said smiling. "A little. Mrs. Winters."

"What have they told you? About my wife?"

"Yes. Diana. In Washington. Very beautiful. Not very
happy with life or the diplomatic routine. Your son in
boarding school. Enough to know you are well anchored.
But then, so am I. On paper, at least," she said, again with
a half smile. She wanted things to be equal between them.

"Maybe I didn't want to know much more," she said.

"Do you feel like talking now?" She sat straight up and away from him. "About your marriage."

"Like many," he answered, "it's been sustained mostly by inertia. Plus the institutional support of various diplomatic communities. I go for days now without even thinking about Diana. I don't say that with any pride. . . ." How long, Anna wondered, since she last gave Sam a moment's thought? "To the surprise of very few of our friends," Shepherd went on, "my wife chose to stay on in Washington when I got the Budapest post. My years of secrecy and silence made our transition to life apart pretty smooth. She's got her tennis and her bridge and, these days, more and more. . . ." He looked away and did not finish.

"She was a lovely woman," he said with a proprietary smile. "Though it was her sense of humor I really fell for. Lord, she could make me laugh! It's mostly sarcasm now, the wit that first held me like a magnet. Though she can still do very good imitations of various State Department windbags."

"The times," he said, looking almost defiantly at Anna, "seem to have passed over her brand of country-club beauty. And me with the times, I guess."

"You're trying to put me off," she said. "Aren't you?"

"Don't be silly. Why would I do that?"

"Because this scares you," she said. "*We* scare you. What I want to know," she began, "is how somebody gets to be a spook."

"God, I hate that word," he broke in with a scowl.

"Somebody like you," she pressed on, "who reads literary magazines and learns dead languages and isn't trying to prove anything. How?"

"My God, you sound like a War Crimes tribunal," he

said. "Anyway, my darling, I don't usually answer that question. Or I answer it in a way that wouldn't satisfy you. Glibly. What is it about you? This desperate need to *know* things? Do you know what a risky business too much truth is? I've stopped asking questions myself . . . makes life so much simpler."

"Simpler, maybe. But I don't see simplicity as my overall purpose in life. . . ."

"What if I don't *want* to tell you how it happened . . . how I became what you choose to call me?"

"I would not regard it as a sign of great trust," she said, prepared for a gamble. "It would not be a great thing for us . . . whatever 'we' are . . . whatever future we might have. . . ."

"My God, are we talking about the future already? You, a married lady—Diana in Washington, granted, but no talk of divorce. . . ."

"We don't have to talk or even think about the future. I can enjoy these evenings with you for what they are . . . the nicest times I've ever had in bed with anybody," she said with an artificial brightness. "And that should be enough. Anyway, I'll soon be off on another . . ." Her voice was giving her away, slipping, slipping into whimpers. Then she couldn't shape words anymore for the whimpers were a cry from some deeper part of her. Her shoulders shook and she buried her face in her arms which hugged her knees. She felt as cold and more alone than the night Uncle Pali had taken her to the opera, to *Rigoletto*, the week her parents were taken away.

"Oh Lord," he whispered, "oh, please don't cry. I can't stand to see you like this." He folded his arms around her bare shoulders. "I didn't mean to hurt . . . I'm just not used to talking about . . . those things . . . and you are so . . . demanding. Emotionally, I mean."

"It's just that . . . nothing is fixed anymore. . . ." She hated herself like this and strained for composure. "There's nothing certain in my life." She felt her eyes getting full and hot. Though she knew it wasn't just Shepherd she was weeping for; already she feared life without him. "I need you," she said very softly. "I think I probably felt your rightness for me the first minute I saw you slumped in that chair in the lobby waiting for me. You looked so detached and I've never been able to pass up a challenge. The plan was for you to fall in love with me, you see. And now. . . ." She stopped and breathed deeply, for she felt used and angry with herself. "Dammit all, how could I let this happen?" she asked with heat. "Let all these expectations build up?"

He started kissing her palm, her shoulder, and then her neck. "Anna," he whispered, "oh, Anna." His mouth traveled down her back and this made her moan softly.

"Do you love me, then?" she asked, still safe in his arms.

"I love this . . ." he said, his hands running down her breast to her thighs and not moving from there. "This is our world. But I dare not love you."

"Does that mean yes?" she asked, warmed by a surge of love and humming now with the warmth and the possibility of him.

"Yes," he sighed. "Yes. It means yes." And kissed her hard to stop her from asking any more.

Twenty-eight

CHRISTOPHER," SHE WHISPERED. "Darling, are you asleep?" He thought he was dreaming so he did not stir. She kissed him gently on the cheek, and the warmth of her made him turn over and reach for her. "I haven't slept at all," she murmured. "I've been watching you for hours, it seems. It's almost daybreak, and I want to talk to you."

"Talk to me? Now? Good Lord, Anna, don't you ever quit?" But he sat up, touched by the look in her eyes. "What is it, Anna?"

"I want to know something because . . . well, because it's important, that's all."

"All right," he said, rubbing sleep from his eyes.

"When you called me . . . the first time, I . . . it was a professional call, wasn't it? You already knew about me. My background. My parents' time in prison. You even knew about my father's deportation and what that did to him, didn't you? No. Let me finish. You thought you could find out more about his friendships. Right? This was why you wanted to get to know me. Don't interrupt. Please. There are things going on here . . . I can't quite get a handle on them. Poland . . . there's going to be trouble . . . and you . . . wanted my help. And now. . . ." Her voice was hoarse with insomnia and he felt a pang for her anguish.

"I guess I never wanted to talk about any of this," he said sighing. "I suppose I'm not really surprised you put it all together. You're too good a reporter."

"The fact is," he ran his fingers through his disheveled hair, "I really didn't expect this to happen. This," he shrugged, "need I seem to have for you . . . I must be getting old." They both fell silent for a long moment. "It's what I do, Anna," he said at last. "I have no choice in the matter. There was a time when there was more to it than that." He sounded bone tired and looked his age for once.

"Christopher," she spoke at last. "It's okay. As long as you really feel this way it's okay. I needed to hear you say it. I guess I've used you too, in a way. You've listened and you've soaked up some of my confusion . . . and hurt . . . a lot of other things. You seem to understand things without any words. I love you for that. But it's very important for me that we deal honestly with each other. There hasn't been a lot of that in my life. Honesty. Do you understand that?"

"You see," she began, for the look in his eyes reminded her of something, "I still remember what they did to him. My father. I saw what the AVO had done to both my parents. I have tried for a long time to forget. Now I know I never will. Just as my parents never got over what happened here. I was there in court. They broke them, Christopher."

Twenty-nine

I T WAS HER LUNCH BREAK. Anna's classmates
were scattered in ragged disorder around the playground.
The little girl sprang to catch a ball heaved from the opposite
end of the asphalt. She caught it, looked up with a smile of
victory, and saw the two men. For a moment she clutched
the ball against her chest and did not move. The other
children on the playground stepped back, away from her.
There was no sign of the teacher. One on each side of her,
the men led her toward an unmarked car. A driver sat behind the wheel, its engine was running. Anna let the ball
drop as her guards shoved her into the back seat.

Minutes later, she was in another courtyard. This one
belonged to a former high school which now served as the
Supreme Court of the country. She saw them before they
saw her. Her tall father's military bearing slumped into an
old man's gait. His face looked blotchy, his eyes were swollen. Though it was a mild winter's day, he was clinging to
his overcoat. And his hair! His smooth black mane looked
as lifeless as a wig and was streaked with gray. The expres-

sion on his face made the child shiver. It was the look of a
man who has stopped caring—a dead and beaten face, without any light coming from the eyes. Until he saw Anna.
"Mommy! Papa!" Arms and legs flying in every direction,
she ran toward her parents. Her father scooped her up and
held her head tight against his face. He did not want her to
see his own tears, but she felt his face wet against her own.
"Anna, Anna, my little girl," he repeated over and over.
"How could they bring you to this place?" He sounded
shocked, but there was relief too in his weary face at just
seeing her.

She looked at her mother. Julia looked just like pictures
Anna had seen of her grandmother in her fifties. Her lovely,
wide eyes had sunk deep into their sockets, ringed by dark
circles. Her complexion had a greenish tinge. She did not
smell of Arpège anymore, but the stale smell of prison. For
this reunion with her husband, she had done something to
curl her lank hair. Prison toilet paper for curlers? The hairdo
only accentuated her haunted appearance.

The Bators were each flanked by a uniformed guard and
a non-uniformed, State-appointed lawyer wearing matching
expressions of boredom. Her parents weren't allowed to
stand closer than three feet from each other. Anna could tell
how bruised they were by each other's appearance. They
did not look at one another, but only at her. "You look so
grown up, Anna," her mother whispered. "So healthy!"
The little girl looked back in wide, dry-eyed amazement.
For they did not resemble her parents at all.

Their guards led them inside to the court's waiting
room. Anna was placed in the hands of a red-haired matron
who kept one large, fleshy hand on her shoulder. Its moist

warmth seeped under Anna's black cotton pinafore and made her squirm. The room smelled sickeningly of disinfectant. Anna was afraid she would be sick. Her parents' faces remained impassive, as if they no longer noticed such things.

Suddenly, the doors of the courtroom flung wide open and two jailers appeared, their automatic pistols trimly belted, their faces as clean of expression as spectators at an overlong ballet. Between the two guards, the shrunken form of a prisoner in striped uniform, unshaven and handcuffed, spoiled the guards' picture of robust health. Anna turned away. As a child, she somehow always equated ugliness, decrepitude, and ravaged old age with evil. (The influence of wicked witches and spinsterish stepsisters in the literature of her childhood.) The guards were crisp and clean, certain of their right over this victim. Were they on the side of Good?

What about her parents, then, who looked more like the wretched prisoner than the guards? Again, she felt divided in her loyalties, ashamed of her ambivalence. She saw her mother and father exchange glances as the prisoner passed in front of them. It was a look that said, "They haven't stripped us of our final layer of dignity. We still have our overcoats."

Even a child could see that this was not to be a real trial. It was a well-rehearsed, polished performance by a cast that knew exactly what was expected. A lawyer who broke new ground under cross examination of the accused would have been ridiculously out of place here, like an actor who suddenly starts improvising his lines midway through *Romeo and Juliet*.

Only the ghostly pallor of the accused, the unseemly slowness of their movements, marred the crisp efficiency of the rest of the performance. It had taken this obviously well-oiled machine with all of its cogs and wheels six months of hard work to achieve the Bators' day in court.

The courtroom's walls were an acid green and decorated with the outsized portraits of Mátyás Rákosi. The leader's large, shiny head and hooded lids were a photographer's nightmare, but a cartoonist's dream. Rákosi was, once again, after a brief fall from grace, back as Party Chairman. His portrait was flanked by the sainted, muscular semi-profile of Lenin and the bushy-bearded classic of Marx. Looking at those portraits, Anna felt embarrassed to think she had admired them in Zsuzsi's home as the sober messengers of a better world. They were so clearly lined up against her parents. She despised their expressions of smug superiority and hoped they had not brought her here to help their case against her parents.

The shades on all the windows were tightly drawn. The only sound was the drone of the fluorescent light overhead. Her parents sat on hard benches and waited. AVO officers (Anna knew them by now from their burly chests and eyes that moved like searchlights) disguised as municipal police hugged the walls.

"Please rise," the court usher announced the arrival of the three judges. They would soon become three familiar faces from scores of Anna's childhood nightmares. First to mount the dais was Comrade Judge Judith Kalmar. In her mid-thirties, she had pleasant, homely features and majestic posture. She looked in Anna's direction with just a moment's surprise. It appeared she had forgotten this particu-

lar, and obviously exceptional, detail of the trial. Anna tried
a tentative smile on her, to see if, perhaps, the comrade judge
was also a mother. Judge Kalmar's eyes narrowed in vague
irritation, as if a mosquito had landed on her snub nose.

Antal Dinyes, a man who seemed to possess no neck,
followed. His jutting jaw let all know he was a man accustomed to the exercise of quiet authority.

István Zold, raw-boned, bespectacled holder of dual
Soviet-Hungarian citizenship, followed his comrades. He
nodded in the direction of Anna's parents. "Be seated," Zold
declared, unblinking eyes frozen on the accused couple.

"Alexander and Julia Bator," Zold intoned with calculated boredom, "have you any objections to the composition of the court?" This was 1955; Socialist legality was the
order of the day. The letter of the law was scrupulously
upheld, whenever it was deemed convenient to do so. The
accused had no objections.

"Alexander Bator, you are charged with subverting the
People's Democracy and committing dangerous crimes
against the State under Section I of Article 70 of the Criminal Code of the Hungarian People's Republic. How do you
plead?"

Her father, painfully frail, still clutched his overcoat at
his throat as he pushed himself up from his seat. The room
was so still. Anna heard her own breath, which sounded as
loud as an old woman's wheeze. She wished she looked as
beaten and sluggish in her movements as her parents. Anna,
with her plump, rosy cheeks and well-pressed school uniform, felt like a gaudy thing in that sickly green room.

She smiled at her father, a contrived little smile to make
him feel better and to make him proud of her amazing

courage. As though this were a typical field day for a six-year-old: to sit in court and hear the State call her father and mother traitors. But she could not pull it off. She started sniffling, at first very softly, muffling her sobs with the back of her hand. Then loud, messy tears washed over her, and she no longer saw the dry, green room or smelled its antiseptic odor. She felt the red-head's tight squeeze on her shoulders and arms and heard her father's soft, "Guilty as charged, your honor," as she was pushed out the door.

She was no longer there to hear her mother's guilty plea to the same list of crimes. By the time the matron brought her back, the atmosphere in the courtroom had brightened perceptibly. The three judges looked as proud as if they were accepting the thunderous applause of an invisible audience.

"The State has heard from expert witnesses confirming the testimony of the prosecutor," Zold concluded. "The members of the court will now adjourn to decide under the procedure set forth in the governing constitution of the Hungarian People's Republic, a verdict in the case of the State vs. Alexander and Julia Bator. The court is now dismissed."

A fatherly smile played on the parched, thin lips of Comrade Zold as he swept past Anna. She read there a look of complicity. He seemed to be telling her that between the two of them they got their guilty pleas. She despised him for that look, would have liked to shout or beat her fist against his chest, but understood she could not.

They were all led back to the prisoners' antechamber to await the verdict. Alex sat on one bench with four guards and Julia and her team were on the opposite side of the room. Anna's guardian still had a hand on her shoulder and kept her at a brisk pace as she walked between her parents. Anna was quite convinced they would all be permanently reunited very soon after their joint performance in court. Composed now, she turned back and whispered, "Mommy, Papa, I love you," before she was prodded out the door to the waiting car.

But they were not freed for a year and half after this family reunion.

Thirty

INSIDE THE DARK VESTIBULE, a lurid yellow reproduction of Van Gogh's *Sunflowers* hung in place of the photograph of Stalin lighting his pipe.

"Come in," the stoop-shouldered man with dull brown eyes coaxed. His voice, like his posture, seemed to hover uncertainly between two possibilities. "I was sorry to hear about Zsuzsi's death," Anna said, and followed him toward a pair of faded stuffed armchairs that stood in front of a curtainless window.

"Yes." The old man sighed and pulled his pale blue terrycloth robe tighter around his middle. "It was a stupid accident. She was less than a block from home . . . A Fiat screaming around one of those famous Roman piazzas . . . It was my last post . . . I've retired now from the Diplomatic Service. Zsuzsi had her heart set on seeing Rome before I came home." He gazed out the dirty window. The Diplomatic Service, Anna thought; what a multitude of sins it covers.

Anna wondered if sorrow or time alone had softened

everything about the arch villain of her childhood. For a
moment, she could not recall why she had felt the need to
pay this call. Searching the retired secret policeman's eyes,
she suddenly remembered Zsuzsi's eyes, brown and unblinking, fixed on her, goading her to answer the door to
four men who had come to take her mother away. But now
Zsuzsi was dead and the secret policeman had been reduced
to this: a pensioner in a terrycloth robe.

"We are so happy with the way things worked out for
you and your parents," Lieutenant Rona said. His pigeon-
colored hair hung in thin slices across his forehead.

"You can come and play with Zsuzsi any time," the
voice, resonant with implied menace, echoed from her childhood. "We prefer, however, that she not visit your apartment." Until the day when Zsuzsi's assistance had been
enlisted in the smooth execution of Anna's mother's arrest,
the Bators' apartment had been enemy territory. Anna had
been overjoyed to finally show the older girl her room that
afternoon.

"I read in a magazine about your new job," the lieutenant said. "About how you can pick and choose your overseas
assignments now. Very impressive," he said, lips pursed in
paternal approval.

This faded little man in a room smelling faintly of old
age had once filled her with terror. Where was the stiff
bearing, which even when cloaked by a nondescript dark
suit, had once hinted at a uniform?

"Would you like something to drink?" he asked, rubbing his bony hands together. "I'm sorry it's so chilly in
here. They keep it this temperature during the day . . . not
many of us in the building then." It had an odd ring, the

lieutenant's "They." For Anna *he* had always been "They."

She had come, she supposed, seeking the simple, energizing hatred this man's name had once stirred in her. The emotion was lost to her, washed away along with the lieutenant's straight shoulders, hard brown gaze, and the photograph of Stalin, lighting his pipe.

"I . . . I have to be on my way," she said, rising.

"Yes," the pensioner was on his feet, a little too fast. His relief was too spontaneous. In the old days he never showed any emotion beyond bare condescension. Why, Anna wondered, does nothing last? Not even hate.

"My wife will be sorry she missed you," he said in a neighborly way, leading her toward the dark front hall. "Of course she still remembers." He stared at his slippers.

Anna also remembered. The lieutenant's wife, eyes swollen and hair for once flying in every direction, had rushed into their apartment, called her father by that discredited bourgeois title, "Herr Doctor, please!" She blubbered through her tears that they would surely hang her husband, Erno. It was the first time they had ever heard the lieutenant's first name. The Revolution was four days old. "There are lynch mobs in the streets. You know they will find him." Mrs. Rona looked pleadingly at Anna's mother. "I am a mother. Please hide him."

For five days, while the Freedom Fighters searched cellars and attics for the hated AVO officers, the lieutenant was hidden in a closet in the Bator's bedroom. The apartment was never really searched. Alex Bator himself had been released from prison only days before. He was already back reporting on the Revolution for *New Day* magazine, something of a hero to the Freedom Fighters. "We don't need any more blood in the streets," her father had said quietly. "There has been enough hysteria in this city. One kind is no better than another."

"I hope it goes well," the lieutenant said, rubbing his stiff fingers together, "your homecoming."

Descending the steep hill of her old street, Anna felt a wave of gratitude. Lieutenant Rona had evoked for her the memory of the gallant man who, throughout her childhood, had tacked lightly above the surface of other people's hysteria. It was the way she would have liked to remember him.

Thirty-one

THE OLD MAN rose slowly from behind an elaborately carved dark mahogany desk. "*Szervusz*, Anna, Hello," he greeted her, as though they were meeting not for the first time. He did not embrace his old comrade's daughter, but directed her toward a worn, blue couch. "You are enjoying our beautiful city?" he asked without the least interest in her reply. Anna instantly perceived he was a man openly impatient with social niceties. She guessed he made a profession out of this uncouthness, being no threat to those in the front. A man who blooms in the shadows.

She studied him momentarily. His raw, peasant's face looked as if its lower half belonged to a different head altogether. The chin and the lower lip were askew, the neck, corded by veins, as though it had all been hurriedly assembled. Andor worked his jaw forward, sideways, searching for comfort from obviously ill-fitting dentures.

"I had heard about this homecoming." he said, giving an ironic twist to the word. "I hoped, sooner or later, you would get around to seeing me." She wondered how fully briefed he was on her comings and goings. On Shepherd.

"I feel as if I know you already," she began, feigning a confidence she did not feel. "From all my father's stories," she lied.

"You look a great deal like him," he said. "The eyes. The cheekbones." A split-second's warmth coated his voice, but the eyes which appraised her struck Anna as dead, immune to either beauty or suffering. He looked like someone who had experienced so much personal pain, perhaps witnessed so much of it in others, he had no sense for shades of feeling or emotion.

"What is it?" he asked. "You are cold?"

"No. It's all right. Thank you." She tried to control a shiver.

He had the sort of presence that immediately reduces the temperature of a room, she thought. As if someone had left a window open. Already she was certain of one thing: this man was no friend of her father's.

"Does he still fence?" he asked.

"Oh, no. Just a mild game of Saturday tennis now." She smiled. "The establishment game."

There is no one left to challenge him to duels, she thought. Nor are there any causes to make him toss a glove in the face of a genteel thug. Alex Bator's ghost hovered over the Persian carpeted office of Kadar's counsellor.

She sat quietly, her hands expectantly folded in her lap, biding her time, letting him take her measure. "Chairman Kadar," she began tentatively after a while. "His health is . . ."

"As good as can be expected for a man his age," Laci Andor said gruffly. "Who has not had the benefits of a quiet

life. And who hasn't time for the 'establishment game,' as
you call it."

"The text of that editorial in *Nepszabadsag* . . ." she
paused, waited for his reaction. Lines gradually cut his forehead. "The one about Polish revisionism," she said with
false confidence. "Hardly in the spirit of the fragile new
détente both Moscow and Washington seem to be working
toward." Andor shifted his jaw from side to side. "Jaruzel-
ski's absence from the group . . . Kadar's pained look . . .
What does it all mean?"

"We are happy to have you here in Budapest," Andor
said finally. It was not a speech of welcome. "Do not make
the mistake of confusing two systems, however. Yours and
ours. You are too smart to forget that though you are now
an American television reporter," his eyes bored through
hers, "you are also our guest." But his tone was even and
mechanical, he could have been talking to a perfect stranger,
not Alex's child. "Bear in mind the difference between our
two cultures as *they* sometimes did not. They loved the
West so much." He did not need to name her parents. "I did
not agree to see you for the purpose of giving you what you
would call a 'deep backgrounder.' I am a busy man, Anna."

"I am not asking any privileged information from you,"
she pressed on. She was no stranger to slippery officials or
the glib salesmen who were often their aides. "It's no secret
Solidarity is an embarrassment to the Kremlin and a head-
ache to the rest of the Soviet Bloc." She saw him wince at
this, as if she had just uttered an obscenity. "But there is a
long history of real friendship between Poland and Hungary, isn't there? A friendship that goes back much farther
than the current . . . ah . . . political line-up. . . ." She stopped,

her mouth felt dry. Andor had stood up. Anna was accustomed to lies, denials, even personal insults flowing from the mouth of authority. She had never before encountered anything like the glacial expression on his face.

She felt a surge of heat rising in the back of her neck. In her eagerness she had committed the unpardonable sin of questioning a man unaccustomed to the most ordinary function of Anna's profession. She had momentarily forgotten where she was and under whose rules she was playing. She sat now like a chastened child, afraid she had abused an opportunity. Andor did not walk out but continued to stare out his window.

"In some ways," she said, desperately trying another tack, "you probably knew my father better than I ever will." She suspected that much was true. Slowly, Andor eased himself down again.

"The fact that the two of you went through those terrible times together . . . while I've only known him in comfortable times. Well, I mean, since we left. . . ." Her voice trailed off awkwardly. He smiled at her embarrassment. The dentures he displayed seemed much too large for his mouth. "You knew him in different times," she said.

"You could say that." He smiled a half smile. "I knew Alex when things weren't so good for him. Or me." He leaned back in his armchair, beginning to savor the turn of the conversation. "Oh, he was ripe for something, believe me. He was pretty open for suggestions for kicking the old order in the teeth."

"Tell me about that . . . about him," she urged, though she tried not to sound too pleading.

Something flickered in the gray man's eyes. Did she

remind him of something, an expression perhaps that took him to a place that only existed now in the dimmest corner of his memory? She was certain nostalgia had nothing to do with his reminiscences.

"Yeah," he said, breathing in. "He signed up with us. There was no more brutal way to break with everything he had stood for than signing up with us. We weren't even a subject suitable for social conversation in those days. It was better to speak of sex than about Communists in polite company before the war," Andor said with some pride.

He fished out a pipe from the pocket of his jacket. With agonizing slowness he went through the ritual of stuffing it with tobacco, lighting it, drawing deeply on it before poking it some more. He did not strike Anna as a "busy man." He seemed in no hurry. As Party elder, perhaps he no longer needed to exert himself for anybody. Anna sensed that Andor had outlived the fiery orators who could ignite a crowd but who did not have staying power. He had probably survived them all by being plodding and totally loyal and a threat to no one. Or playing that part with consummate skill.

"We liked each other." The words had an odd ring in his mouth. "Don't ask me why. Everything was turned upside down in those days. There was a mutual need . . ."

"You mean . . ." She stopped herself. "Was he a good . . . ah . . . a good Communist?" Anna asked, bluffing to encourage Andor's confidence. The word "Communist" when attached to her father sounded stranger to her ears than had she asked, "Was he a skilled acrobat?"

"Communist? No. I would not have called him that. It was a marriage of convenience. He needed us. We needed him. He did some useful work for us." Andor shrugged. "With him, you're never real sure what's going on inside. That much hasn't changed, or you wouldn't be looking at me with those big eyes. Right?" he asked, again without expecting an answer. "When he wanted out," Andor said, "we let him out."

The half hour was ticking away and she waited nervously for Andor to glance at his watch. Suddenly, he rose to his feet and she, sagging with disappointment and frustration, followed. He shook his head, however, and motioned for her to sit down. He lumbered out of the office and Anna heard him tell his secretary, "Ring Szabo and Kocsis and set up a morning meeting instead. They only waste my time with useless gossip," he mumbled, returning and closing the door behind him. He sat down again, without looking in her direction, lost in his own thoughts.

"I'm the one who got him to confess," he said as simply as if he were announcing that tea was being served.

"Yes," she gambled. "Confess."

The old man seemed to have summoned up another world. He was no longer preoccupied with his pipe and even seemed oblivious to Anna's presence. His bent frame was buried in an outsized tapestry-covered armchair, a legacy, no doubt, of the days when this same building served as the dual monarchy's Ministry of External Affairs. Dusk gradually enfolded the city, and still Andor had not turned on a single light. The semi-dark seemed to match his mood.

The penumbra, like the years, softened Andor's coarse features, blurred his grainy complexion. In the silvery light, she could barely make out the coarse lips which still gripped a pipe, now gone cold.

"That's what you came for, isn't it?" he stated simply. "Alex was never one for opening up. Not to his friends. Not to his family. Not about anything that mattered. He didn't trust anybody." He shrugged. "He had his reasons, believe me."

"I always thought that someday he would tell me," she said.

"Ach." Andor's impatient hand cut through the dark, dismissing her simplicity. "For him, silence is the only acceptable form of communication. It would be a mistake to make him talk. There is too much . . .

"It must have been shortly before daybreak . . . ," Andor picked up a different thread. "Alex figured it to be about five in the morning." She thought at first the old man was hallucinating. But as he continued, she realized he had begun a tale that, until now, Andor had kept as closely guarded as the other betrayals he had been party to.

Thirty-two

ALEX SAID it was the time he most despised. Just before daybreak, Andor recalled. "A lifetime to kill before he was swept up by the day's routine." The stillness made Alex feel he was the last survivor of an apocalypse they hadn't told him about. Reluctant to admit he was awake, he didn't move. Only his numb fingers, ice cold from their prescribed position outside the inmate's blanket, worked themselves slowly back to life.

Then a scream, high-pitched and shrill, shot like an electric current through Alex's limp body. "Assholes!" Someone had the courage to shatter the prison's proudest achievement: an atmosphere of serenity found nowhere else outside a Swiss sanatorium. The lunatic's ravings set in motion the muffled, felt-footed army of peacekeepers. A quickness in the air, the clinking of delicately inserted keys, followed by the gentle closing of a cell door told Bator the angry prisoner was getting a hearing.

Alex pondered the identity of his brazen neighbor. He waited in the silence for another clue. "Bastards!" The next cry, another piece in the puzzle. "They don't know who I am!" So now the Colonel was himself an inmate. The ferret-faced little man who had been the brilliant stage manager of every major show trial from Rajk to Mindszenty and scores of others no one outside the AVO had ever heard of.

Fodor had once enjoyed a reputation in Budapest as a first-class cobbler. He had fashioned immaculately fitting shoes for Alex himself. But the shoemaker tired of making others look sleeker and more elegant than they really were. He yearned for the kind of respect that only fear stirs in the hearts of men.

Once the Communists came to power, there was only one certain source for that kind of authority: the secret police. The former shoemaker ultimately built the AVO's finely tuned machine from its first cog up, made it the eyes, ears, and sword of the State, made every reasonable citizen tremble at the sound of those three deadly letters. It was the fantastic fulfillment of the cobbler's pipe dream. The barbed wire, the watchtowers, the baying hounds were all part of his army, and only the visible portion of his vast empire of fear.

Alex had seen the shoemaker slip quietly into the court-room during his own trial. He saw Fodor occupy an incon-spicuous back bench during the same performance Anna had also attended. But the Colonel stayed only long enough to establish his credentials as Worker of Miracles and to show the Bators he had not lost his touch. That was his style: quiet, somber, cameo appearances, momentary and mysteri-ous, at events staged by himself. Fodor was a sort of Hitch-cock in his own productions. Alex Bator knew the applica-tion that had gone into those productions. He knew of the blunt memos. He had seen one on his own interrogating major's desk. They spelled out the deadline for a prisoner's capitulation. Fodor's deadlines had never been missed.

The sound of the Soviet National Anthem suddenly washed the entire prison in its jaunty beat. The guards had finished their morning inspection. Full of martial spirits, they set off to fulfill their day's contribution to the Dictatorship of the Proletariat.

A key turned in Alex's door. Andor's slumped figure moved into the half light. "Alex, the Party needs a traitor," Laci said flatly. "I've come in the name of the Party. You must confess. The Party needs your confession."

Laci did not look much healthier than his old comrade. But the red-rimmed eyes that were fixed on Alex gave him scant comfort.

There was little the two men didn't know about each other. Each knew the depth of the other's obsessions and frailties. Only Laci, however, was in a position to make use of Alex's. Andor had survived the bloody purge of non-Moscow-bred Communists that followed on the heels of Stalin's break with Tito. His fingernails had not resumed their natural growth since his eighteen months in the hands of the AVO. Electric shocks had been used to encourage his own rapid confession. He had emerged from prison six months after Stalin's death, a shuffling, stoop-shouldered old man of forty-two. The Party, he was the first to tell you, had few more loyal servants.

Laci admitted frankly the Party soared high above the requirements of friendship. The Party was his reason for existence. Life itself! Without it, he knew he would have remained a moderately successful mechanic, certainly not a member of the privileged New Class.

"Don't you feel like a slug sometimes?" Alex had once asked Laci in that haughty tone he occasionally still affected with him. "A slug fixed inside the pocket of the Revolution. Wherever it goes, whatever twists and turns it takes, so do you."

"You're the only man who can pull off this one," Laci persisted. "You've convinced everybody you're Phelps Lewis's best buddy. The West's eyes and ears in this vast wasteland! For how long now?"

"Ten years," Alex replied, his voice cold, lifeless. "Ten years on Easy Street." He had filed reports to the Party on unstartling conversations with Ambassador Lewis (whose own butler could have performed the same task with equal zeal) and occasionally gave his American magazine pieces a certain gentle shading so gentle the far-off reader was perhaps not even aware of it. Alex knew all along that in time the Party would have more ambitious plans for him.

"It was the summer after the Liberation," Laci recalled. "That's when Comrade Rákosi suggested you make yourself available to one of the capitalist news agencies. Well, it was only fair, after that nice little outing to Geneva to meet that faggot Englishman. Cut pretty deep into our budget in those days, take my word for it. But there's no one in the Party who could have done the job as convincingly as you."

"You were the messenger that time too, weren't you, Laci?" Alex looked up. "Christ, he's brilliant at choosing the right man for the right job, your Comrade Rákosi. Isn't he?"

"Look, Alex," Laci finally sat down on the prisoner's

cot, "I know what it's like. I've been through everything you're going through," Laci, his eyes ashine with conviction inside their watery frames, gripped Alex's arm.

"You know as well as anyone," Alex sounded as if each word required a superhuman effort, "I'm not burdened by too many ideals anymore. But one thing they cannot get out of me, not after more years than I care to account for, is a confession of treason. That is one of those rare crimes of which I am innocent. Forget it, Laci. Tell your pal Rákosi that is not how I wish to be remembered by future generations of misguided fools and idealists." He ran his fingers through his still thick, unkempt hair. "You've already got a piece of my hide. Go someplace else for your damn confession."

"Alex, you've got it all wrong!" Laci interrupted. "You're not going to make your name as traitor to the Party. Just the opposite. That's why I'm here. You're going to *serve* the Party. And the people who count will know. They'll remember when the time comes. Believe me." Laci's brow was beaded with a damp mist.

How well Alex Bator knew that the Party came down hardest on its own. Somewhere, Arthur Koestler had written that ideology brings out the most destructive side of a man. Rajk had found out. So had Kadar and Laci himself. Now it was Alex's turn. He hoped his superiors were surprised by his staying power. He had not caved in as quickly as scheduled. "You thought I'd be a soft target," Alex said with a half smile, "because I don't wear your baggy suits. You thought I'd dance to any tune for a little peace and quiet. God," he sighed, "I'd give my kingdom for a cigarette right now." Laci had come prepared. He handed Alex a pack of his favorite English brand. Alex lit one and filled his lungs with as much smoke and nicotine as they could hold.

"So they've coated the pill with a little sugar, is that it, Laci?" Alex turned to the man who still shared his cot. "Confess, and we'll guarantee you a place in the Party's Hall of Fame. I guess that means I'm not yet completely dispensable."

"It's a hell of a lot more than a little sugar, you cynical bastard. It's a chance to play a part in a high stakes game. In Geneva." Laci uttered the word reverently.

Geneva! Alex thought. Again. "Oysters and the Ballets Russes and I'm still paying the bill," he mumbled.

"You know I really envy you your certainty, Laci. I get the feeling you still believe in the same things you were ranting about in Barcelona. You were so sure then. I was sure of nothing. Tell me, did I really buy some of what you were selling? Seems a long time ago . . ."

"There is nothing else," Laci's voice was low. "Not for me. There never will be."

"Let's get off this subject. Living according to one's principles is pointless stuff. Come off it, Laci. Do you really think anybody can afford to do that for more than a few short months between adolescence and whatever the next stage is? But one thing they won't get from me is a phony confession."

He had heard the confessions of too many others. They always thought they would save themselves. But they never did. Their reward was either a long prison term or death. Once the Party had your confession, you became useless.

Alex made up his mind six years earlier, during the trial of Josef Cardinal Mindszenty, that if his turn ever came, they would not break him. He had covered that nauseating affair for *New Day* magazine. It was a public trial; the eyes of the world were on the squalid little kangaroo court. A black-robed, scarlet-capped prince primate of the Roman Catholic Church stood in the dock. Alex Bator, raised a Roman Catholic, had expected the old man to stand up to them. Mindszenty had neither wife nor children, only a two-thousand-year-old Mother Church which had always embraced martyrs. Yet when the ludicrous list of charges was read, the bowed cleric, his long face sullen and gaunt, could only say, "I voluntarily admit that I have committed the acts which I am charged with according to the penal code of the State." And off he was led to solitary confinement. For how many years?

Alex had decided he would do better. His spirit may have snapped like a dry twig over the years, but he was constitutionally still a brave man. That, like his bone structure, was a genetic inheritance. Now, his old comrade was presenting him with a scrap of hope. There was a third route between the punishment his body and soul had endured in the last weeks, and simply caving in. Laci dangled a shred of self-respect before his nose. An illusion of service. Duty. God, he was tired of the whole charade.

"The fact is, that ten years after the Liberation," Laci droned on, "the Imperialists are still not willing to live in peaceful coexistence with us."

"The unfortunate thing about you, Laci," Alex cut in, "is that you no longer have the capacity to speak like a normal human being. It all comes out in Party jargon. Maybe after all these years of spreading their gospel, it's become your truth? Maybe you haven't got any questions left? C'mon, is that really possible? Tell me?" For some reason Alex wanted to be convinced. Had it worked on at least *one soul?*

But Laci had come with a prepared message from which he would not depart. "There is every sign the Eisenhower-Dulles clique is working to wrench Poland, East Germany, and maybe even Hungary away from the Socialist brotherhood," he plodded on.

"For Christ's sake, Laci, you don't really believe . . ."

"Hold it, Alex," Laci stood up, "you haven't been monitoring Radio Free Europe the way I have. Okay, I know it's not among your prison privileges, but believe me it's absolutely inflammatory stuff. Night after night, they're practically promising to send in the Marines if the people rise up against their oppressors. That kind of primitive propaganda."

Alex was beginning to understand his "historic" role in all of this. "I've been chosen to lend credibility to the rumors of internal subversion, haven't I, Laci?" Laci nodded in exuberant approval. The scheme was brilliantly simple.

"You have, no doubt, already begun diligently spreading these rumors of Western infiltration. Let me guess. The *New Day* correspondent, a Hungarian national, and Phelps Lewis, the American Ambassador, don't really play bridge on Thursday evenings. They're exchanging information. Doing the reconnaissance work for the job Langley will finish. Right? That's why I was picked up on the way home from the Lewises, isn't it? It all fits very nicely. All I have to do is sign on the dotted line. The Party's reliable Mr. Fixit." He stubbed his cigarette out on the floor so hard it looked like Shredded Wheat.

"With the Politburo's full recognition. That's the one big difference. You've been picked by Comrade Rákosi to help smear egg on the Imperialists' faces at the Geneva Summit," Laci said, offering Alex another cigarette.

"Deeply honored," Alex replied, holding his cigarette to Laci's light. "But forget it."

"All right, Alex, all right. Calm down. We haven't run out of ideas yet." Laci narrowed his eyes. "I guess we kind of thought you might pull this stunt." He shook his head. "You never really were one of us. Nobody had illusions on that score. So," Laci breathed deeply, as though pained by what he had to say, "here it is. Say yes to the confession, and you're guaranteed safe passage to the border. You, Julia, and Anna."

"What?" Alex whispered. "What did you say?"

"You heard right," Laci said with a scowl.

"You mean you'd let me go? Why?" This was one possibility he had not dared contemplate. Wasn't his existence too entangled with the life of the Party to allow dreams of anything else?

"What the hell." Laci shrugged. "It'll give Khrushchev a chance to show how forgiving he can be. Letting a confessed spy off, scot free. Don't worry, he intends to get something in return. Something a hell of a lot bigger than you, my friend."

"Laci," Alex looked hard into the man's expressionless eyes, "they'd really let me go?"

Laci stood up and knocked twice on the cell door to signal the guard the call was over. "Sure," he said without turning back. "Why not?"

Thirty-three

ANNA WAITED ANXIOUSLY as the silence between them deepened. Then, seemingly refreshed by a new stream of memories, Laci shifted in his chair and picked up his tale.

"Our flight from Moscow was rough," he told Anna in a tone that was more confident and grew strident as he neared the story's climax. "There wasn't much conversation aboard the official plane. Anxiety you could taste." The twinengined Ilyushin lumbered to a halt at the end of the Geneva International runway. The pilot adjusted its bulky frame to the space not already claimed by two sleek four-engined transports: one emblazoned with the gold crest of the Royal Air Force and the other with the white and blue seal of the U.S. Air Force One. "So the British prime minister, Anthony Eden, and Eisenhower, were already inside the terminal," Laci went on, "waiting for our delegation."

A rotund little man with rosy cheeks and a broad, predatory grin bounded out of the small plane first. "This was Nikita," Laci said with a condescending smile. Khrush-

chev's suit had been carefully chosen for his first confrontation with the Western Imperialists in their territory. Stalin
had been dead for two years, but his legacy of paranoia
thrived. Khrushchev's suit of pale mauve looked as though
his tailor had a weakness for films of the Chicago under-
world, circa 1940. His wide-cuffed trousers flapped in the
breeze off Lac Leman. (Laci Andor couldn't keep the zestful
contempt a survivor reserves for a non-survivor out of his
voice.)

He was followed by a short, goateed figure, a striking
contrast to the Ukrainian peasant. Nikolai Bulganin was the
straightman to the crude comedian which was among
Khrushchev's preferred roles. Bulganin's taste in clothes had
even more remote antecedents than his colleague's. With his
white overcoat that swept the tarmac, he looked like a char-
acter in search of an Italian opera. Bulganin was the nominal
head of the Soviet State. "But we all knew better," Laci said.
The cautious climb to supreme power of the Party Chairman with a fondness for barnyard humor was well under
way.

Eyes downcast and seemingly oblivious to his surround-
ings, the Soviet Foreign Minister, Vyacheslav Molotov, de-
scended with measured steps. His banker's three-piece suit
and pince-nez made Molotov look as though he had stumbled into the wrong revolution. Lenin had once described
him as "the best filing clerk in Russia." Bourgeois exterior
notwithstanding, Eden and Eisenhower were about to experience the depth of Molotov's commitment to Stalinism.

No introductions were necessary. All parties to the
Summit had met in Moscow before the Soviet occupation of

Eastern Europe. "In those days, you see, all of us still toyed with the illusion of friendship," Laci explained with a dry laugh.

The formalities quickly dispensed with, the delegations were swept by Swiss security into their long line of black, bullet-proof limousines. The Americans were the last to roll out of the airport. "I'll never forget the Secret Service agents, grim, dark-suited men, like a bunch of undertakers running behind the long Presidential car," Laci shook his head, "which looked like a submarine."

Khrushchev, on his first trip abroad, broke tradition by parting the opaque white curtains that usually shelter Soviet leaders from the intruding eyes of outsiders. "He was not about to let a single detail escape his attention," Laci told Anna. "He knew Geneva was Europe's nursing home. A place for bodies, nerves, and institutions to convalesce." Exiled emperors and terrorists (before they were transformed into statesmen) had chosen Geneva's sober affluence as their springboard to violence and revolution. Vladimir Ilyich Lenin, long before he became a golden icon, had gathered strength in this decorous haven.

The Chairman shielded his eyes from the piercing rays that Mont Blanc's peaks reflected off the lake. "Frankly," Laci continued, "he suffered from a bad case of nerves. The sight of the impeccably tailored, icy Anthony Eden and the tall, grinning General had made him pretty self-conscious of his own baggy clothes. Plus the Anglo-Americans' planes didn't help matters either. They made the Soviets' look like an embarrassing relic. Stalin had predicted that after his death the Imperialists would eat up his heirs like so many chickens. Khrushchev was not about to offer himself as a meal for either the English aristocrat or the American President."

Khrushchev did not need an agenda to know the subject uppermost in the minds of Eisenhower, Eden, and Edgar Faure, the French Prime Minister. (A pleasant fellow, the Russian thought, but not much point in cultivating him, given the revolving door that was French politics under the Fourth Republic.) The reunification of Germany was what brought the Western delegations to this tranquil corner of Europe. "Reunification was nothing but a euphemism, this we knew, for the withdrawal of Soviet troops from East Germany. A naive dream," Laci explained, "a sign of how little the West understood the Soviet Union's justified fear and resentment of Germany. We, on our side, were equally determined to use this Summit finally to legitimize the existence of the German Democratic Republic."

It was Eisenhower's suggestion that after the first afternoon's session the delegations wash away the day's tensions with martinis. It was the moment Khrushchev had been waiting for. He had not wished to show his hand in the formal atmosphere of the plenary session. For this crucial testing of his mettle, he had done more than order a new, statesmanlike suit from his tailor.

"Mr. President," the little man bent close to the American, nearly sweeping the General's shoulder with his nose, "I do not see how you can expect us to negotiate in good faith," Khrushchev noted with satisfaction the number of quizzical wrinkles on the President's brow, "when only a short while ago, the Hungarian People's Republic was forced to arrest two of your spies, masquerading as journalists. Your ambassador was, of course, involved. What was the name of that couple, Comrade?" Khrushchev cued his Hungarian aide, Laci Andor.

"Bator, Comrade Chairman," Laci replied. "Alexander and Julia Bator. They will be tried on charges of espionage for the Imperialists." For a split second the hero of the Normandy landing looked perplexed and troubled. Khrushchev thrust out his chest and savored the moment.

"In the spirit of Geneva," the rosy-cheeked little man beamed goodwill, "we shall escort your spies across the border. They're all yours! *Prosit!*" Khrushchev raised his glass to the General.

"The scheme gained us a razor-thin edge at the conference," Laci Andor concluded. "After this, things began to look up for me. . . ."

Thirty-four

A WAITER IN a stained white apron majestically presented them with the steaming platter of veal stew. "*Köszönöm,*" Anna said to him in Hungarian, "we'll serve ourselves." The sticky, sad strains of an old Gypsy tune, one she remembered had been her mother's favorite, floated from a violinist's strings. Tears streamed down Anna's face. "That proves you're Hungarian," Shepherd said with a smile, and reached for her hand across the table. She had faithfully reported to him the details of the long meeting with Laci.

She withdrew her hand, felt far away from him at that moment. "Anna," he asked, "where are you?" There was genuine concern in his voice.

"It's just a little bit more than I bargained for. Isn't that obvious?" she asked sharply. That moment she had a strong urge to spill something very cold or very hot in his lap. "You knew," she said, "everything Laci told me, you already knew. Didn't you?" He did not answer. "Why didn't you tell me?" she demanded "Why Laci? Why did I have to hear it from him?"

"Don't forget about your own life, sweetheart," he said, as soothing as a doctor. "You have the right to make your own set of mistakes, you know. And not live in the shadow of theirs. For heaven's sakes, don't let this become an obsession."

"How can it not become an obsession?" she asked in a reedy voice that was not her own. "They have guaranteed that it becomes just that. God, no wonder I felt as though I were someone's invention, a flimsy thing without the flesh of a *real* past. My past . . . *their* past is mostly an illusion." She stopped. "So you also know that my father's obligations to the Party . . ."

"Were declared null and void," he interrupted. "When they escorted you to the frontier. Payment for services. A year and one half later than promised. Yes," he nodded. "I knew. Now you have your history, Anna. Or most of it," he went on. "And you could drive yourself crazy trying to figure out their motives. You and I will probably never understand the sort of wild faith that led them to think they could bury it forever. That you would never piece it together." Shepherd shook his head. "They're coming from a different world, Anna. A different century. And they are probably trying to protect you from . . ."

"No," she interrupted him. "I don't believe that they were only shielding me. It's more complicated than that. Because *they* were. *He* is."

"You know, they think of themselves as such good Americans," she said, "and yet, they failed to see the most important thing about being American. That you can stop hiding your past. That's the whole point! It's okay to be just about anything. Anything but a Nazi. In fact, the heavier your baggage, the better. The more you are respected for getting there. How could such supposedly worldly people be so naive?"

Naive. One of her father's preferred invectives. "A naive man," he would say of someone whose simplicity he could not suffer. Someone without subtlety or finesse. She had always heeded those indomitable judgments of his. She would have to let go of his standards. Who was he anyway?

"He filed reports to the Party," Laci had told her, "occasionally gave his American magazine pieces a certain gentle coloration. . . ."

That coat of immunity her parents had worn during the chilliest days of the Cold War had been purchased at so high a price.

So was the price Anna was paying for gaining a history. It had to do with trust and the cushion which parents provide against all else. She could not put this into words for Shepherd. And the truth was that others always seemed, well, *ordinary* next to her father. Sam. Even Christopher Shepherd. Even while she despised her father's silences, she had been deeply moved by them.

What was Shepherd compared to the pull of flesh and blood? Compared to her father, who had admonished her in a letter from prison, "Anna, you must read Dickens. Start with *Little Dorrit.* And then Kipling: *The Jungle Books.*" The most terrifying thing about that letter had been her father's spelling mistakes. He, the strictest of taskmasters about spelling and grammar, misspelling words that even a schoolgirl could spell. What had he seen in there? For there was hardly a word about his own nightmare. Now she knew. "Weeks of battering," Laci had said, trying to squeeze a confession out of him. (When all along they had an irresistible "final offer" up their sleeve: Passage West.)

Later, in America, her father would groom her first clumsy attempts at English composition. Late in the night, after he had filed his own reports. One day he told her, "You don't need me to look at your writing anymore, Anna." His vowels seemed to harden and flatten with the years. "English has become more your language than mine." This left Anna with a vague sense of guilt, for she knew he was quicker and funnier in his own language. He had left the most poetic and the most courageous part of him behind.

Shepherd with his complacent, arctic blue gaze knew nothing of this bond. Her father had been her lifelong safety net. His persistent demand for more out of her, always more languages to learn, more people to meet and conquer. More style. More poise. Pushing her, urging her, goading her to penetrate yet another sanctum. Applauding her. Her tireless trainer for the 1500-meter dash of life. He had been her ultimate line of defense against failure. For if her father, with his exacting standards, cheered, then she stood strong. He was lost to her in a mist of deceptions and deletions.

"Maybe illusion is the only way to survive certain systems," Shepherd said, as if reading her thoughts. "Endless playacting may be your last refuge, once hope is smashed by fact," he mused.

"Yes, but what about when you leave, when you get a chance at another life? It seems to me you should be able to leave the playacting behind then," Anna said.

"Yes, of course you *should*, but can you? Do you think it's possible once you've caught a glimpse of certain things . . . can you ever let go of a suspicion?" he asked, and Anna wondered what sort of things Shepherd had glimpsed along his way.

"Well, I think I've let go of certain things. I've started a new life."

"Ah, yes, but you were a child." He smiled paternally. "You left it all behind you. You are an American. And *they* made this possible. Besides which," he narrowed his gaze, "have you really let go?"

He was right, of course. Why was he always right? She had not in fact let go of those images he called "glimpses of certain things." The faint echo of the hard knock at the apartment door. The blurred image of the blank-faced messengers of doom. The sepia print of the pretty judge with the upturned nose who had no patience with a child's need of parents. Had she really let go? She felt bruised by these moments as if by a childhood infirmity that occasionally reasserts itself in later life with a mysterious ache. Otherwise would she be here?

"I need to see him," she said finally, not looking at Shepherd but out the rain-splattered window of the restaurant, to the river. The Danube, which flows into the Black Sea and eventually empties into the Mediterranean. Budapest closed in on her with its history, now her history as well. "Anyway, they've sandbagged me at the Radio-Television office, Comrade Fekete's empire. For some reason their initial enthusiasm for my presence has evaporated."

"Don't take that entirely personally," Shepherd said matter-of-factly. "It's partly a general nervousness in the air . . . the editorials about Poland . . . and partly to do with . . . other things."

"Like you and me?" she asked, with sudden comprehension. "God, I've been so wrapped up in my own world. . . ."

"You're allowed," he said, "for a little while at least."

"I've got to get word to Levin. I haven't talked to him in weeks," she said and picked up her bag. "Apart from my calls to Sarah, I haven't used the local phones once. See? Aren't I a promising recruit for you?" There was a dry edge to her voice.

"Not even in jest," he said. "I don't like that talk. Anyway, I shall miss you," he said with a forced smile.

"What's this? Sentiment?"

"Did you ever think," he asked, "that maybe I'm as exposed as you are? For one thing," he said, running his fingers impatiently through his thinning hair, "I'm nearly old enough to be your father."

"But Christopher," she said softly, her anger spent. "What are you protecting?"

"A great many pieces of myself which you have never even guessed at. Which you may not find as heroic as the carefully chosen ones you've been allowed to see."

"My God, don't you think I can put the rest together? Or do you see us as James Bond courting Lois Lane?" she asked without humor.

"When we have more time," he said as they stepped into the soft drizzle, "I'll tell you some things about me. About this house I once saw—near Aix-en-Provence—thick with the most amazing blue flowers. Some day . . ."

"Wisteria?" she asked.

"How did you know?" he smiled.

"I don't know. But I do know why I fell in love with you in the first place."

"For me, it was all lust," he said turning her toward him. "For God's sake," he said, "don't make me spell out all the time what I feel. I'm no good at it. And dammit, I'm too old to learn," he added gruffly.

"You know a part of me doesn't really want to go," she said, and kissed him softly on the mouth. What had life been like before her return to Budapest? Her greatest concern last year had been whether she would merit the coveted assignment of floor reporter for one of the two presidential conventions.

"Come back," he said, slamming the door of her taxi. He watched as it turned toward the Chain Bridge and vanished in a gray line of snub-nosed Trabants and Ladas.

Thirty-five

DAWN BROKE QUICKLY. One side of Anna's plane was bathed in hazy blue while the other framed a fiery ball floating between black horizontal bars. By the time she landed, thick clouds had spread over the Rhine Valley for the day's duration. The typically gray, dismal day and the bone-penetrating damp of North Rhineland harmonized with her mood.

She drove blindly down the Bonn-Cologne Autobahn, indifferent to the flat, smog-choked countryside, the puffing refineries which tore by in rapid succession. The suffocating provincialism of the German capital did not irritate her this time.

One thing she had learned in the last few weeks had to do with places and memory. She had been sentimental enough to think she could somehow merge with the landscape of her childhood. She knew now these places did not retain a memory. They had moved on, shifted their loyalty. And, in the long run, so had she.

The garden of her old house, where she had first heard

the word "Jew," after the initial shudder of recognition had become just a neglected patch of grass and earth. Other little girls had probably slept in the same corner of "her" room and dreamt their own wild dreams. And what did she have in common with the inhospitable residential blocks that surrounded her old church?

She knew now she would never walk those streets as anything but a pilgrim. No, her connection to Budapest was freighted with less tangible, vastly more disturbing ties than rooms, trees, and cobbled alleys. She had been so simpleminded. "Going home." But how could she have known?

Of one thing she was glad: her father was safely out of Laci Andor's reach. "He was well rewarded for his guilty plea," he told her. "Your safe passage across the border, a year after the events of '56," Andor's euphemism for the Revolution.

She drove past the Israeli Embassy in Bad Godesberg. Its jumble of barbed wire, the helter-skelter nest of aerials and satellite dishes, a deliberate assault on the landscape. This embassy made no concession to the pastel and gold puff-pastry architecture of the rest of the turn-of-the-century spa town. Should she feel some connection to this fortress? Her grandfather had once patched a yellow star to his overcoat. Yet she could squeeze out no emotion. She felt strangely abstracted, floating above reality. What was real when so much had turned out to be made up?

She had flown to Bonn, the closest UNS Bureau to Budapest, to speak to Abe Levin on a secure line. The Bonn Bureau's ambiance matched perfectly any one of the network's other half dozen overseas operations. Anna surveyed the dreary scene, as disheveled as a restaurant right after closing. The Bonn crew must have just retreated to another location.

Net air shipment bags and black video cassette boxes labeled variously *Rush:* ex Moscow to London, ex Paris to New York, ex Frankfurt to Jo'burg, littered the industrial gray carpet and molded steel desks. They also decorated the Rome or the Hong Kong UNS bureaus. An abandoned, pockmarked dartboard hung on the wall for camera crews whiling away hours between assignments. The windowsill was littered with styrofoam cups, cesspools of cold coffee and ashes.

This was not so much an office, she thought, as a clearinghouse between locations for correspondents, producers, and crews. They had become more or less interchangeable parts, moved around the map by managers who ventured out of the five boroughs of New York only as far as Westchester and Fairfield counties.

Only one corner of this neon-and-chrome wasteland was animated by flesh and blood. Fräulein Angela Ritter, one hundred and thirty-five pounds of compact Teutonic womanhood, had occupied a corner desk for twenty years. Though she did not fit the network's image of sharp-edged, aggressive youthfulness, not even the steeliest of New York executives had the temerity to dislodge her from that position.

"Fräulein," as she was universally known, had been hired as a cuddly, sweetly dim secretary by the first UNS Berlin correspondent. He, like several of his successors, enjoyed Angela's ample curves between vague murmurs of an imminent trip to New York and bigger things.

Twenty years later, still no trip to New York had

materialized. Nor did Fräulein, curves now solidified into geometric permanence, any longer elicit such flights of fancy. Angela's once pleasant features were now set in an expression of reproach. There was no one, however, in the entire UNS overseas operation who had penetrated the mysteries of airline schedules more fully than Fräulein Ritter. Nor did anyone else have her instincts when it came to satelliting out of a remote Punjabi village or an African swamp.

Without ever having left her office, Fräulein was on first-name terms with every satellite station operator from the Atlantic to the Urals. Collectively, they had made possible the American viewer's familiarity with the major wars, famines, and coups of the last two decades.

"Grüss Gott, Angela." Anna smiled and extended a hand over Fräulein Ritter's IBM Selectric. "Wie geht's, denn?"

"Na, ja, es geht," she answered with a deep sigh. "Look. I'm the only office manager in Bonn still without a computer. CBS and ABC both went over last year." She looked up at Anna with an expression of unlimited suffering. "They keep telling me it's on order."

Anna knew the slightest encouragement from her would release an avalanche of the latest New York perpetrated injustices. So she asked brightly, "Got anything for me, Angela?"

"Ach, ja. They're all waiting to hear from you. The Morning Show. Radio. Even Abe Levin's secretary has called. You seem to have forgotten the world back there in Budapest, nicht wahr?" she said in a tone of mild reproach, and handed Anna a pile of telexes.

"That's what I'm here for," Anna answered, and headed with her messages to the correspondent's desk across the room.

"Anna: Welcome Back to the Free World," the first telex read. "Need situationer on upcoming West German elections. Xplain in min. half why Great American Public should give a damn. Soonest. Regards. Morris."

Once, not so long ago, telexes had made her blood pump faster, with their promise of new places and unpredictable characters. And above all, air time! Now the prospect of yet another breathless race from the editing room to the satellite feedpoint back to the bureau for late night word that New York either loved or did not love the piece only made her stomach tight with anxiety.

She picked up the thin text of Hungarian history she had bought before leaving Budapest. *The Nazi Years*, the shoddily bound tome was called, and was clearly meant only for the eyes of a student cramming for an exam. The cover was a grainy photograph showing Adolf Eichmann, with his narrow fox's face, alighting from a long, shiny car. She flipped the pages idly. "In 1944, there arrived daily at the railway siding at Brezinka several trains consisting of about fifteen wagons." She read the dry Hungarian text, as cleansed of emotion as a museum guide. Bözsi's voice rang in her ear. "I saw Alex cradle his mother in his arms. I think that was the last time I ever saw them . . . any of them."

She read on. "Each of the wagons held about one hundred persons . . . the wagons were emptied, the men being separated from the women and children. The new arrivals from Hungary were told they were to be taken to the bathhouse. . . ."

Anna gazed absently out the window of the Pressehaus office in the poured concrete media-government compound. A stocky couple wearing matching Tyrolean suits strolled by. They radiated good health and unassailable self-confidence. The man and woman kept an even, measured pace, as if in time to a distant melody, accessible only to themselves. Green hunting hats trimmed with small tufts of boar's hair bobbed up and down in mutual recognition. These Rhine strollers used to strike her as picturesque remnants of a gentler time, as harmless as animated cuckoo clocks. She was sickened now by the sight of those little green hats going up and down, confirming the robust health of their particular civilization.

A word returned from her childhood: Deportation. Like the refrain from a song, she had heard it again and again. So often that the word had become as bloodless as a corpse in a mortuary. As a child she had thought of deportation as a temporary condition: people shipped off to do rugged manual work in the countryside. It sounded almost therapeutic. For in the fifties, everybody seemed to have a father or an uncle who had been "deported" for having the wrong notions or clinging obstinately to old ways. Her parents had described those who never returned in a similar vein: deportees. A vague and open-ended condition. Deportees to Hitler's camps? Members of her own family?

They had spent more time discussing the Wars of the Roses than World War II around her family's dining-room table. Anna knew far more about Voltaire than about Wallenberg. For many years this lapse did not bother her particularly.

"The men stood in one column along the ramp," the

book went on, "the women and children in another. This procedure was accompanied by weeping, and cries of people who were afraid of being parted from one another. The people had to approach the SS doctors in turn, and they decided on the basis of their external appearance on their fitness for work. With a movement of his hand, the doctor directed some to the right, some to the left."

They had never talked about any of this before. Images from hackneyed TV docudramas now intruded on her family's most private nightmare.

She slammed the book shut and picked up the telephone. "Abe," she spoke over the transatlantic hum, "it's Anna." She had no trouble picturing Levin, safe behind a well-trimmed Pound Ridge lawn and walls of properly weathered shingle, deep inside his favorite leather chair, screening tapes. "I've rebased to Bonn. And I need a favor." Levin ultimately saw everything that went out on UNS air. He was a man of legendary energy who regarded sleep as a mark of weakness and made sure none of his people overindulged in it. He was also one of the few genuinely creative minds in an industry that does not normally reward originality.

"What's up, sweetie?" he asked laconically.

"I need to get back to New York. A couple of days of personal leave." She swallowed hard. He said nothing. "It's a family matter and it can't wait. I really can't make much more sense out of it for you than that." One thing she knew, Levin would have allowed her time off to deal with an unwelcome pregnancy with more enthusiasm than for Anna's real reason.

Levin was not a man encumbered by either principles or personal loyalty or any goal higher than the best Nielsen ratings on the books. But he was the sort of executive who would bend or even break rules if he thought you were worth UNS air time.

"Sounds like I don't wanna know. Anyway, it's so quiet out there, I can hear the grass grow by the Rhine. Just don't take too long."

"Thanks, Abe," she said, breathing easily again. "I don't care what anybody says. I think you're a human being."

"Flattery will get you nowhere."

The line went dead. Anna breathed deeply. Then the harsh jangle of the phone roused her moments later. "Hello," she answered in a voice one decibel above a whisper. "My God, the very last person I would have expected. You sound close."

"At the Dreesen."

"You and Hitler have the same taste in hotels," she said, recovering from the shock of hearing the voice of Zoltán Boros.

"Yes, he and Chamberlain had tea and Sudetenland in this salon. The place has lost none of its charm."

"But what brings you here?"

"I'm actually in and out of this deadly village several times a year. They enjoy my little sermons on building bridges to the Behemoth. Can you be at the Tulpenfeld in about twenty minutes?" he asked abruptly.

"Yes." Anna was mystified by the call, but relieved at the diversion it provided.

She drove back on the Autobahn toward the Tulpenfeld and thought again how ludicrous was this town's posture of capital-in-exile. The aggressively temporary feel of the ministries, the obvious lack of care or planning, the great stretches of sandy ground run to weed, all meant to emphasize impermanence. The red-hot glare of the letters CDU and SDP, the two National Party headquarters, glowed against the low, black skyline, like certain hotel signs in the down side of Baltimore.

Anna never felt comfortable in bars. They struck her as forlorn and inadequate shelters against loneliness. The Tulpenfeld had loneliness shellacked to its walnut paneling. There were never more than a handful of customers scattered around the room. Despite its handsome carpeting and rich upholstery, it had all the warmth of a railway terminal. Middle-level government bureaucrats from Delhi and Bucharest, deflated after a day spent peddling arms or grain, nested here at night. Their superiors dined inside pastel mansions, warmed by inviting fires and good Rhine wine. Here a Turkish waiter behind the bar rubbed endless shine onto wineglasses nobody used, for this was a group that preferred Scotch or vodka. Like a Brueghel tableau, with each figure looking into a space of his own, the Tulpenfeld's customers each carried their own transparent bubble of solitude.

Anna had no trouble spotting Zoli, as crumpled as a piece of used tinfoil, in one of the corner booths.

"Anna, come, sit." He sounded effusive and, at the same time, intimate, barely containing his pleasure at seeing her.

"Why do I have the strange feeling you are here not to lecture the Bundeskanzler, but to have a drink with me in this depressing bar?"

"Clever girl," he said, fumbling in his baggy jacket. "Is your bag big enough for this?" he asked, pushing several sheets of paper, rolled into a cone held by a rubber band, into

Anna's lap. Without thinking, Anna shoved it into her large leather shoulder bag. "I would have no objection to your father having a look at this," he said in a voice that was uncharacteristically flat. "As well as yourself, of course."

Before she even had a chance to shape a question, Boros was on his feet, shuffling unhurriedly out of the artificial intimacy of the dim bar.

Thirty-six

S HE AWOKE without a memory of where she was or why she should be there. Every muscle in her body throbbed from the narrow airline seat that had girdled her for the past four hours. For an instant she could not recall why a heaviness of spirit should match her body's ache.

Gently, she squeezed past her neighbor's knees (please, she prayed, do not stir and begin again to regale me with your contribution to the Paris Air Show) and slipped into the washroom. Was it only the ungenerous light of the mid-Atlantic dusk that reflected a middle-aged woman in the mirror above the chrome sink? Her high cheekbones looked sharp, and lines she had never noticed framed her mouth and eyes. Wasn't it too soon for this? She let a weary hand skim her body to confirm that there, at least, youth waged a gallant campaign for survival. No spare flesh, no bags or lines there. "The packaging," they would call it on Madison Avenue. She had stopped worrying about it in the last few months. Her face, her clothes, her image had all been left behind in the city she was now approaching. This was not a homecoming.

She thought about Shepherd. Already, she missed his effortless, soothing gentleness. His fine hands and tired eyes. She had caught a look in his eyes as she left him, a look she had not seen before. In the harsh neon glare of the Pan American 747 washroom, their relationship struck her as askew, fed too much by her gaping need, nourished by her fear of being alone. Without Sam, her reliable tormentor. She was not yet willing to concede the loss of her father.

There would be time for Christopher Shepherd. For now, she needed the *possibility* of him. She needed to miss him and to think about making love to him. She had lately shed so many layers, left herself deliberately open to pain to fill a hollow space.

Thoughts of Shepherd reminded her she had not yet examined the papers Zoli had thrust upon her. My God, she thought, whatever happened to those killer instincts which made her lead the show once a week and earned her obscene calls and even an occasional death threat? Back in her seat, she slowly worked the rubber band off the rolled sheets. The paper was coarse, the typing offcenter. She envisioned soft and hasty steps from a conference room to a supply cabinet, where a pair of large and gnarled hands clumsily worked a Xerox machine without turning on the light.

She stared vacantly at the Hungarian text, too technical for her immediate comprehension. She read and reread the words, forcing her mind to clear itself of its jet-lagged haze.

"Marshal Victor G. Kulikov, Supreme Commander of the Warsaw Pact Forces," she read, "chaired a meeting of the Combined Supreme Command of the Pact Forces in

Zossen-Wunsdorf, near East Berlin. . . . Front staffs from the High Commands of Soviet Forces in forward areas as well as three staffs already in existence within Soviet territory have been formed. . . . The Hungarian Army Staff Headquarters will be located in Székesfehérvár, near the Austrian border." The notes went on to describe military maneuvers that were under way in all points of the Eastern Bloc: in Hungary, Czechoslovakia, Bulgaria, and the German Democratic Republic. On the subject of Poland, the terse message was simply: "Poland's fuel and ammunition stocks are to be transferred to the other Warsaw Pact Forces for the duration of the exercise." There was much more detailed information about river-crossing operations, armored exercises, and amphibious assault training. "Western electronic surveillance of the deployment," Anna read, "will be impaired by the use of advanced electronic screens to cover troop movements."

Anna squeezed her memory for another such staged "exercise." It was in 1968, when the Warsaw Pact maneuvers ultimately merged into the very real occupation of Czechoslovakia. She remembered the smokescreen of disinformation, *dezinformatsiya*, which preceded that invasion. Editorials about "hostile forces trying to force Czechoslovakia off the Socialist Road." Again she recalled the editorial in the newspaper left by her table in the Budapest café. "Not a single Communist can or will agree with those pseudo-theoreticians who forget the class nature of the movement. . . ." She remembered the Brezhnev Doctrine, that child born conveniently in time for the invasion of its neighbor. The Doctrine spelled out the limited sovereignty of the members of the Warsaw Pact, an alliance for maintaining

Soviet domination over its members. Had a clenched fist already pounded on a polished conference table somewhere in the Kremlin, accompanied by a single, definitive word, *khvatit?* Enough.

So Shepherd's fine nose had picked up the scent. This was the final proof he needed to confirm his worst fears. But Anna was one hour from Kennedy Airport and her father. And Shepherd was on the other side of the earth, ignorant of her rendezvous in a dreary bar in Bonn.

It was strange that Zoli, the shrewd political animal, should choose her father, a former Party operative, to receive such sensitive information. Laci had made very plain, however, what it took to win Alex's cooperation. Graphic, in fact. She could begin to understand why he had never told her of his former affiliation. His old comrades were still in power. There was a clear danger involved there. Besides, he could never have become an American citizen with that on his record. This part she could begin to understand. If only her father would start dealing honestly and openly with her. Starting now. Maybe it wasn't too late for them.

Thirty-seven

I'LL GRAB A TAXI at Kennedy," his daughter had said on the phone. "Pan Am is always late. I hate the thought of you waiting." In fact, he liked waiting for her. It was one of the few things he could still do for her. Pick her up at the airport. Her tone was different somehow. Less solicitous, more telling than asking. Alex Bator walked slowly over to his typewriter and realized how little he was looking forward to his daughter's visit.

Whatever illusions of freedom he had allowed himself in the last years had evaporated in the past month. His nights were crowded with memories of things that had happened so many years ago. He had thought, foolishly, naively, he was free of them. He would have to pay the price now. For his own reasons, Laci was seeing to that. Delayed payment for having denied the claims of the past. For Julia's and Anna's sake. And, well yes, maybe for his own. For a few years of . . . surely not happiness? He did not know what that meant. Peace, or maybe just serenity. To live like everybody else finally.

Anna did not think it was enough. Anna, with her simplicity. That hunger. Fine qualities in her world, perhaps, but not in his. Anna would bring them both down. He was powerless to stop her. He could not say to her, no, you cannot go back there. Anna, the cocky American reporter, would not understand. His survival had been a fluke anyway. That kid who drove the camp delivery truck: it was all his doing. And Julia's.

He had been assigned to a camp detail working in the village bakery of Kistarcsa. Alex couldn't remember how he had struck up a conversation with Pista, the boy (he couldn't have been more than sixteen) who drove the bakery van. He was a surprisingly astute and decent sort. Like a lot of people, Pista was confused and embarrassed by the strange new order. He began calling Alex Professor.

Pista liked the Romantic poets of the last century, and there was very little Alex did not know about Hungarian poetry. After a while, Pista smuggled him cigarettes and salami.

"I leave here at six tomorrow," Pista told Alex one morning, "for my Buda run." He tried to sound casual, as though absorbed by sucking bits of bread from between his teeth. "Hop in the back," he said under his breath, indicating his truck with his head. "Stay as quiet as a loaf of bread till I bang on the side."

And so, Alex did. What the hell. He hopped out of the bakery van on a quiet residential street. The sun was shining, the sky was a cornflower blue, and the houses looked like palaces to him. He felt like a man released from the hospital after a lengthy struggle with a terminal disease. The drunken feeling of being able to go in any direction nearly overpowered him. He had lost the habit of making choices. And he knew he gave off the phantom-like air of an escaped convict. Disheveled and lice-infested. It was an act of will to make his legs move briskly.

He knew his luck wouldn't hold out. He made his way to the one place he thought he would be welcome—Julia's. They had met at a dinner party at a mutual friend's home two months and several lifetimes earlier. Julia Foldvary was the daughter of one of the capital's most respected surgeons, respected in part for his enthusiastic support of the anti-Semitic laws.

In a way, Alex regretted that the old doctor and his wife had died in the sixties, in disgrace. They had been posted to a decrepit provincial hospital, the doctor's reward for tending injured Freedom Fighters during the Revolt. Alex would have liked for his father-in-law to have seen Anna. Anna, the American reporter.

Dr. Foldvary's views did not in the least dampen his daughter's enthusiasm for Alex. Just the reverse. Like Alex, she was an anglophile. She had given him his English name, "Alex." "You don't look like a Sandor," she said of his real name.

She had been no beauty, Alex remembered, as he watched the children in Central Park below. No, she was much more than that. She was alive. And with a smile that engaged her mouth, eyes, hands, and shoulders, every part of her. A near miraculous enthusiasm for life—miraculous, given the time of their courtship. He had never been loved in that totally uncompromising way before.

They knew how little time there would be without ever talking about it. Each night they had closed the cabarets on the Margit Island. Everything tasted sweeter, sharper, because they knew the lights could go out any minute. And, of course, they did go out the night two SS officers rang the bell at his garden gate.

Now, as he approached her villa with its massive oak double doors, its immaculate, honey-colored exterior, he thought, what will she think of a man who has not changed his clothes in weeks? A man who will touch her cheeks with callused hands and a week's beard. A man without a future. Or even the right to exist.

"Your eyes," was all she said, holding him tight. "Your eyes have aged." And then she turned away and would not let him see her face for a while. Each hour with her restored a little bit of him. She thrived on his total need of her. In that end-of-the-world atmosphere, it was more than just love binding them together. She was his world. She was laughter and summer and hope and other things which he thought had been obliterated without a trace. And for Julia, he supposed, he was decency and despair. She was hopelessly romantic, Alex thought now with pride. Like their daughter.

Julia's cramped sitting room was stuffed with furniture and bric-à-brac of friends whose departure from her world she refused to acknowledge. There, stretched out on her sofa, their bodies fitting together in the easy harmony of two people who have decided they were meant for each other, he read to her out loud from *The Forsyte Saga*. The city outside reverberated with the Allies' carpet bombs while Alex and Julia delved deeper into Soames Forsyte's neurotic inability to love and be loved.

"These days will be ours forever," he whispered through her reddish-brown hair, in the tone of a man who neither expects nor is offering more than that. He really did see her as a temporary gift. A loan. He had no right to involve her in a life he himself had no taste for. "Alex," she said, her green eyes alive, swimming with emotion, "I want to marry you." He laughed awkwardly. He had no words for this. "You know I have to go back," he reminded her as gently as possible. "They are still at Kistarcsa."

"You can't just walk back in there!" she exclaimed in outrage. "Hand yourself over to them on a platter. What about me, then? If you don't care about yourself, then what about me? This . . . all this . . .," she said, her arms sweeping an arc embracing the room that had been their universe. He stroked her hair and whispered, "Don't you see, if anything were to happen to them . . . Darling how could I live with you . . . or myself?"

"All right then," she said, straightening up, eyes flashing. She had a plan. "We shall get them out. I've heard stories of how corrupt those guards are. Their loyalty goes to the highest bidder. And," she said, twirling an emerald ring the size of a grape, "I know how to get hold of some cash."

Alex Bator was overwhelmed by this determination. He had nothing to match it. His love was as passive as the rest of him had become. Several hours later, they were in her car on the dusty road leaving Budapest. The road to Kistarcsa.

The deathly quiet of that innocent country road. Julia, so full of excitement and conviction. So full of the future. Julia did not notice this quiet for some time. "What a beautiful day, Alex!" she said, waving her arm out the car window as if to grasp the softness in the air. Julia did not notice that the road was empty of the usual traffic to the camp. For she

had never seen the lines of drab green trucks that used to
rumble in and out of the village, wobbly under their cargo
of uniformed men and their bleary-eyed prey. And what
about the barking dogs? Silence. Perfect, excruciating silence.

Alex could feel his breathing slow down, his mouth go
dry. He knew the meaning of that silence. And, by now,
even Julia had stopped her chatter and started looking a-
round, looking for the guards on patrol. And then, the stillness in which the leaves did not flutter was broken by a distant sound. The long, low mournful whistle of a train. Somewhere, possibly still within the reach of a car. He drove
in a blind, helpless rage in the vague direction of that whistle.
He said nothing to Julia, who saw it all on his face. The fury
and the self-hate.

Thirty-eight

H E's AN OLD MAN, she thought, and wished she hadn't come. The eyes that looked at her with feigned warmth were clouded, old man's eyes. She used to stretch to hug him—his chest a fierce mountain of dignity. Now, he stooped to brush her cheek with dry, colorless lips. "My God!" he said with a forced, hearty laugh, "you are thriving!" She felt embarrassed, as if her youth were an affront to him.

"Seeing Sarah," she said, almost apologetically, "gives me such a shot of life. There's nothing quite like that animal love between mother and daughter. Better than a week in a spa." She thought, wasn't there a time when you and I felt that way about each other? When the touch of your tweed jacket against my cheek was all the world I needed?

"Tea?" he asked.

"I'd love a cup," she said, and noticed he did not bother with the pretty teacups and silver tea things her mother had used. There were two mugs and a much-squeezed lemon on a saucer.

"And the flight? All right?"

"What can you say about eight hours of dry air and dry chicken?" she asked. He is so bad at small talk, she thought. He had always relied on his wife and daughter for that, as though small talk were beneath him. Anna was not going to help him out this time.

"And Sam? He must be happy to have you back?" he asked with a too-bright smile.

"Oh, I don't know," she answered casually, for once without regard for what he wanted to hear. "At any rate he won't have me for long. I don't intend to stay. I mean, with Sam," she said, too evenly.

"Anna," he started in his familiar mix of worldly wisdom and gentle reproof, "he loves you very much. And if he is a little bit . . . ah . . . a little bit insecure about you, maybe he has cause?"

The question implied a moral superiority that she used to cede quite naturally to him.

"I don't want to talk about Sam, Papa." It was the first time she had used the familiar name. It did not sound natural to either of them.

"Well, he is still your husband, isn't he?" His lip curled in irony. "Doesn't that mean a little something? Even in the year 1987?" They were each relying on old habits to see them through, like a pair of swimmers clutching life preservers in a stream full of unknown currents.

"I just feel very far from him. That's all." And from you, she would have liked to have said.

Why doesn't he ask me about Budapest? Why doesn't he say something that matters to one of us at least, she thought. He never made the first step to communicate. But he never really had to; others were usually prepared to spare him that burden. No one ever risked shattering that grave mask, the majesty of his silence! She watched his hands as they piled logs in the fireplace. They seemed smaller. Once they had hidden her entire face. "Anna! Anna!" she could still evoke the shrill voice of the governess, Madame Nicole, sharp as a dentist's drill, beckoning her to lunch or bath. And Anna would leap into her father's lap and use his long, tapered fingers as a curtain while they both waited for the tap-tap of Madame's high heels to fade away.

One day when she was ten or eleven, her father had said to her, "Anna, look, your feet are touching the floor when you sit on my lap." She thought he meant she was too big, too clumsy for such carrying on. She jumped off his knee hurt and afraid he might see her tears.

Already, she was beginning to feel like a child. Was it the decor, the clutter that had slowly made its way from Budapest, inside diplomatic pouches and journalists' crates to the Central Park apartment? Was it the accumulation of all those pictures, artifacts, and faded carpets and their history that cued the child in her to perform according to expectations? She wanted to resist. For reinforcement she looked around for the tarnished silver spice burner whose like had caught her eye on a Portobello Market stall. It was nowhere in the dusty room. Her father, the bravest man in the world, had turned his back on something dangerous; being a Jew. Had constructed a life of compromise and duplicity.

"Don't you want to turn on the light?" she asked, as he seemed oblivious to the fading daylight. Like Laci, she thought. "I saw Andor. Laci Andor," she said abruptly. He had still asked her nothing about her trip.

"Oh," he said, bending down to fiddle with the fire. She kept sneaking looks at his face, searching for something new, a mark of some sort. His high forehead and sharply chiseled nose, the fine, thin lips now pressed together, as if waiting for something to pass.

"Yes," she said. "A strange man. And a hard one." For the second time in her life she now saw his eyes grow wide with an animal fear. "He respects you," she said hastily, dumbly. "Maybe even likes you," she lied. For she was afraid of his fear. "I don't imagine he likes too many people." Her father's lips eased from the tight position into a straight line. "But hearing him talk about you. . . ." She hesitated. She looked out the window at the snow swirling under a street light. She would have liked to feel the snow on her cheeks. "It was hard for me. Since I had to pretend to know so much more than I did. Or do." So now he knew. He still said nothing, but seemed hypnotized by the burning logs. For a split second Anna was tempted to pronounce Bözsi's name. Shake him from his maddening composure. But she resisted, for she did not intend to let Bözsi control this moment.

"Your mother would feel so proud," he said at last. "To see how well you look. How well your career is going." Had he heard her? He had always ducked behind his wife's emotions to camouflage his own. He was doing that now, while trying to steer her to safe ground.

"Yes," he went on, "seeing you . . . here, and when you pop up from those places I have never visited, on the News. Yes, then I know we did the right thing. To have come here." He spoke without emotion, only the accent which had become unusually thick gave him away. She suddenly noticed his jacket. It was made of dark green corduroy and she remembered exactly when her mother had given it to him. Their last Christmas in Budapest. The jacket was made of a fine, soft fabric that had mellowed with the years and was redolent of their family life.

This is a big mistake, she thought suddenly. What have I come for? What do I want from this unprotected, lonely man? What sort of heartless child am I? Sitting here with the calm face of a prosecutor.

"Another cup?" he asked, his face seemingly lighter, less weighted by anxiety than before. He had picked up the change in Anna's mood. Her remorse for pain she had not yet inflicted.

"Papa," she started. Damn. He's giving me what he has always given me—composure, good manners. Transmitting quiet guilt. It's not enough. Not from a father. What about the trainload of ghosts he has been living with? Zoli. Laci. Bözsi. Images of an elderly couple, faceless but surely doomed. Now they are my ghosts, too, she thought. Damn his perfect facade.

"Papa," she began again. "Why didn't you tell me?" Plunging in with both feet was the only way she would ever do it.

"Tell you what, Anna?" he asked, still calm, but no longer smiling.

"That we are . . . were . . . Jewish."

"*We* are not," he answered with a strained smile. "You are not. Your mother was not."

"That wouldn't have mattered much in those days. You. Your parents. Why?"

"Anna, believe me," his face was taut with a forced, benevolent smile, "every family has skeletons in its cupboards."

Whatever she wanted to say was trapped in her throat. She hoped he read outrage in her eyes.

"Maybe if I had looked more like . . ." he started quietly, then stopped. Aware she was pulling back from him. He looked helpless.

"Maybe then I would have felt more like . . . more . . ." He seemed incapable of saying it. What depth of loathing, she thought, must he feel for that mark, to have exorcised it from his vocabulary.

"I admit," he said with a deep sigh, "it was naive of me to think you would not find those people, you with your fine talent for detective work." So it was her fault. The crime of indiscretion. "But people are always eager to shock. Anxious to reveal secrets to anybody who will listen. People, Anna, are, on the whole, not very nice. I have very little use for them." He seemed almost content to have his longstanding habit of trusting no one confirmed once more.

"You always did have a dramatic streak," he said, groping for a light tone. "All this must be a fine adventure for you. Of course, that is a luxury I did not possess in my youth," he added with a sharp brightness that was meant to hurt.

He is throwing a wall of guilt around me, she thought. For what argument could she possibly marshal to compete with what he had been through? And what she, the gilded girl, had not. Only this time, it wasn't enough.

"But my grandparents . . ."

"Anna," his voice sounded conciliatory again. "You are

here, I am here, doing what we are doing, living the way we do, because we have not looked back. We have always looked forward."

"But, Papa," she said, suddenly feeling that she might yet budge the heavy boulder that barred her path. "Nobody can ever threaten us again! This is a different world. You behave as though the world has not changed at all!"

"How naive you are," he shook his head with excessive, patronizing sympathy. He made her feel so small. "Just because everybody has always treated you well, courted you, because you are pretty and smart. That is how we wanted it! That is why your imagination cannot stretch far enough to see how different things could be. As I found out. . . ." His voice drifted off. Anna felt the boulder she had been trying with all her strength to move fall back into place with a thud.

She had nothing left to lose. "Aren't you, in effect, linking arms with *them?*" she asked. "Aren't you, more or less, admitting, the way *they* do, that ours is an inferior segment of humanity?"

"Ours?" he asked with a sneer. "That sounds very strange coming from you, my dear. Aren't you being a little bit of a voyeur? All this vicarious dramatizing? Claiming your right to this . . . this *history*," he hissed the word at her, "without ever having paid a price for any of it." He rose from his place by the fire and walked over to the window. She knew how much he despised losing his temper, how debased he felt by it. He studied the street below and waited for the wave of anger to recede.

"It's wonderful," he said, his voice all control now, "to be able to allow oneself such rich emotions. Such a wealth of high principles and sincerity." He turned and faced his daughter. "Sitting in an apartment overlooking Central Park."

He looked at her with such pained reproach, she knew he wanted her gone. She knew then, a moment had passed that would not come again.

"What did happen to them?" she asked quietly.

"Just what you suspect, I suppose," he answered, all emotion carefully squeezed out of his voice. "Auschwitz," he said, and turned away from her. "That's what you were after, isn't it? Auschwitz," he repeated, and walked out of the room.

Thirty-nine

SHE HAD NOT CALLED to let Shepherd know she was coming. She couldn't, somehow. Oh, she wanted him to be there. But she needed him too much now to risk asking.

The terminal reminded her more of a Greyhound bus station than one of the sleek airports of the West. It had none of the random cacophony, the bustle of last-minute shoppers, idlers wasting time and money of the crowds at Kennedy or Heathrow.

This was a solemn sort of place. The dim waiting room felt tight with unspoken tension. So much was at stake here: the gateway of a country which had only opened its doors to the world by a thin crack. Anna saw grim faces, not yet convinced they would actually board planes for Vienna, Munich, and beyond. Passports could yet be revoked. Someone, someplace could change his mind, place a call, and declare it was a mistake.

Two fleshy stewardesses in polyester suits the color of

rust passed Anna, who waited for her bags to appear on the creaky carousel.

"God, it's great to be home, isn't it, Mari?" one of them said in a voice intended to carry in Anna's direction. "Another French meal and I would burst!" The women were swollen with the self-confidence of those vetted for the country's most jealously guarded privilege: travel abroad. But at least they were "home," Anna thought. Was she? It didn't feel like that. The sentimentality which had blurred her first impressions had lifted like the mist that hugs the Danube each morning and is burned off by noon.

"Auschwitz," he had spat the word at her, as though it were her fault.

A uniformed frontier patrolman, a Kalashnikov like an offering resting in his arms, blocked her way to Passport Control. "Foreign or national?" he asked, barely moving his lips. For just a split second, she hesitated. "Foreign," she answered stiffly.

He continued to study her face, then scanned each line of her passport with the infinite patience of a well-armed custodian of law and order. He had nowhere to go.

Anna felt her nerves, like warm ooze, slide up and down her arms and legs. He stood there and appraised her, an entire system behind him. She was alone. "It's partly to do with the editorials on Poland," Christopher had said. "Partly to do with you and me." Were they waiting for her on the other side? She forced herself to stay calm. There was nothing to be gained by irritation here. Had this guard's father or grandfather worn a cock-feathered cap and riding pants to speed the condemned out of their own country? Her grandparents? At last, he motioned laconically for her to

proceed toward Passport Control. He looked pleasant
enough now, satisfied he had made his point. She hated him
for his effortless ability to make her pulse quicken.

The only one waiting for her on the other side was
Shepherd. He was leaning against a desk that proclaimed:
"Fly Malev Airlines . . . A Taste of Paprika Before You Land!"
They smiled and embraced without speaking. "Good to
have you back," he said softly. "I missed you."

"How did you know?" she asked, trying to keep pleasure out of her voice.

"Oh, we have our ways." He smiled and took her bag.
"Someone else is nearly as pleased as I am about your return." He turned to face her.

"Oh?"

"Yes. Your 'Uncle.' Zoli. He's made several discreet
inquiries as to your whereabouts."

"I don't think it's for the same reasons," Anna said, eyes
automatically surveying the airport parking lot.

"I haven't had a chance to tell you," she began once
inside his car, "but Zoli and I met in Bonn." Out of the
corner of her eye, she saw him straighten up behind the
steering wheel. "He gave me a document. Notes from a
meeting. Things do not look good for Poland. My guess is
Zoli is trying to cut things off at the pass, by getting the
document out to the West. A little preemptive publicity
might reduce the shock of surprise. Maybe even force them
to call off the whole thing." Shepherd gripped the wheel
tight. He appeared to be feeding data into his mental computer, and waited for the answer to flash across some imaginary screen.

"Where is it?" he asked finally.

"Where is what?"

"The document. What have you done with it?"

"I gave it to my father as a parting present. Dropped it on his desk on my way out." She was trying to sound light. "Something to compensate for my visit. His very own scoop. It's been a long time since he's broken a big one."

"Was that three, four days ago?"

"More like a week."

"There's been nothing in any of the weeklies," Shepherd said. "Not a word in the five dailies I read. Did the material look legitimate to you?"

"Yes, absolutely. I think Zoli took a pretty big risk, getting it out." They drove through a neighborhood of bleak, working-class housing blocks. Structures rather than homes, thrown up to meet some functionary's quotas: "Fifty thousand new units were made available to the Workers in 1984. That is four thousand in excess of expectations. . . ." Thunderous applause for this tour de force. Blocks without landscaping or terraces or anything but poured concrete. Night had begun to enfold the dimly lit city in a thick coat of ink black. Children were still hunched over tricycles and old men sat on hard wooden benches, bent over their canes. Anything, Anna guessed, was better than going inside one of those places.

She could feel harsher images of her old country replacing the sentimental ones. She regretted this the way she always regretted the end of the first, misty stages of a love affair. She would have two cities to deal with. The city of her memories, richly poignant, peopled by larger-than-life heroes and villains. And this place—a city of dry rigor, the domain of small-minded bureaucrats. Mean in inconsequential ways. The frontier guard's little game. Lieutenant Rona in his terrycloth robe, the shrunken villain of her childhood. Edith Fekete, the mustachioed empress of Radio and Television. Small fry. Except for one man: Laci Andor. There was nothing diminutive about what he stood for.

"I can't understand why my father's done nothing with that document," she said to Shepherd. "Poor Zoli. He must be crazy with worry. He trusted me. And my father . . ." So had she, of course. She had assumed he would seize those hastily Xeroxed pages and shape them into the red alert which Zoli had clearly intended them to be. Just as she would have done. If her mind were operating in its usual fashion. If she were not pulled in another direction. Distracted.

She would never forget her father's eyes when she finally asked, "What did happen to them?" Eyes that had just seen a ghost. Round eyes, primal in their pain. Eyes that had never been allowed to mourn. Mourning is meant for the survivor, didn't he understand that? For his sanity. Not so much for the dead. Along with other emotions, he had exorcised mourning. Otherwise she would not have caught that wild look in his eyes.

Anna was barely aware they had reached Shepherd's house, parked, climbed up the steps leading to his front door, and stepped inside. In a weary, resigned voice he said, "I really did miss you." There were more lines and a deeper darkness under the eyes. He put his arms around her. "I will always love you." Still she did not speak. She did not know where to begin.

"Is it Sam?" he asked. "Have you two worked out a whole new marriage?"

She laughed. "I'm sorry. But that seems so far out of the realm of the possible. I mean the whole idea . . . it's as if it happened to somebody else. No, Sam has nothing to do with anything. Except, he's Sarah's father. Other things have happened . . . but right now, I'm worried about something else. I'm worried about Zoli." She did not yet give voice to another fear, but went to the telephone.

"Mr. Boros, please." She waited with her hand over the mouthpiece. "God, I feel so rotten about this," she whispered. "He went out on such a terrible limb, for nothing, it seems. Hello," she said, switching to Hungarian. "Yes, I'm back. Thank you, a very nice time. That would be fine. I look forward to it as well. Zoli," she began, but caught a look of alarm on Shepherd's face and remembered where she was. "Zoli, I hope you are all right. *Szervusz*, bye-bye." she said, and hung up.

With a warning finger on his lips, he closed the subject and led her to his sofa. "Tell me about your father," he said. "Tell me how the visit went. Please." She thought there was a kind of intimacy in his voice that had not been there before, as though things that touched her now touched him as well. In her absence he seemed to have allowed himself the forbidden luxury of introspection. The examined life is not worth living, he had told her once.

"I failed miserably. He wouldn't share anything with me. He hates me for bringing it back. He made me feel that. That I was cruel and unnatural to dredge it up. I will never know anything about my grandparents. Except"—she looked away from him; she had never uttered this word in a personal way before and had to mentally rehearse it first —"except that they did not survive Auschwitz." She released her breath and continued to avoid his eyes. "And the rest," she dropped her voice and the words tumbled out, one on top of the other, "the Party connection, the forced confession, the rest of the . . . the fakery, I don't know, maybe I will never know more?" She tried to pretend she was talking about someone else's life, to keep her voice even.

"Well, you had to confront him," he said, gently. "Anybody would have in your place. I would have."

But she did not believe him. She was sure he was much less needy, more able to let things go, get on with life. "He made me feel like a voyeur," she told him. "Do you think I'm a voyeur?"

"Anna," he said quietly. That was his way of telling her that he loved and wanted her that moment. It was their code.

There was a new softness about him. A tenderness as he held her and stroked her hair and cheeks that had little to do with passion. His hands made her feel whole and good. "Oh," she started, "you are so vital to me."

"Yes," he whispered, "and you to me, Anna."

Just then, all seemed right to her. He was right for her. There would be no mysteries between them. No playacting. He knew everything about her. The past and the uncertain present. His hands rested lightly in her lap. She looked down and for a moment could not distinguish between his fingers and hers. Her lips barely touched the line of his jaw. The moment had a beauty and a weight she would only really understand long after it had passed.

Forty

THE SQUARE-SET MAN who seemed to have shrunk closer to the ground in the last weeks shuffled slowly down Váci Street in the direction of the old Astoria Hotel. Spindly trees were already rich with premature buds on this balmy morning. But he did not notice. Zoli's face was shiny from exertion, his breathing heavy inside his creaky, weathered leather coat. The street was still quiet. It was too early for the shoppers and tourists who, during the day, own this strip of boutiques and cafés, to have made their appearance. Still, Zoli turned his head at every soft step behind him. He had started doing that when he returned from Bonn some weeks earlier.

Once or twice, he tapped his inside pocket to make sure it was still there. He had begun to lose track of things—keys, letters, only inconsequential things. Still, his forgetfulness was beginning to erode the bravado that had been his lifelong armor. He touched his pocket one more time and pushed open the revolving door of the Astoria's lobby. He was relieved to find it deserted.

There was a time when this now rundown foyer swarmed with life and echoed with the brisk stride of officers of the Wehrmacht who had set up their headquarters here. The aging, failed writers and poets who used to pass aimless hours in the lobby's cozy nooks were swept out. Henceforth, they were told, the Astoria was in the service of the Third Reich. The Gestapo opened up for business right there in the lobby. Alex once told Zoli of how astonishing it was to see a long line of people snaked around the block from the Astoria. Citizens patiently waiting to provide useful information: concierges denouncing Christians who sheltered Jews in their apartments, Christians reporting Jews for not wearing the yellow star. These helpful bits of information were generally rewarded with either better jobs or larger apartments. A lively place, the Astoria's lobby in the old days. Not these days, thank God.

The marble floor resounded with Zoli's heavy tread. Yes, he had been right to choose the Astoria. The big shots had long since abandoned it for the Hilton, the Intercontinental, or the Forum for their morning coffee. It said something about your position, being seen in those places. Everyone knew they only accepted hard currency. The Astoria, its peeling splendor untouched by progress, its scarred face reminiscent of a burn victim's, had fallen to the lowest provincial apparatchiks. Trade delegations from Pécs or Miskolc, beefy types shoehorned into black suits pushing a new variety of feed or looking for a big time in the capital. They kept the place open. They might even be dazzled by the remnants of gold leaf and the dusty, frayed Persian carpets. At any rate, there was little risk of any of them recognizing either Anna Bator or Zoli Boros.

"There you are," she said, suddenly bursting out of the revolving doors. "Have I kept you waiting?"

"No, no. It's fine. I'm happy to see you," he said with a deep sigh of relief. Speech, she noticed, seemed to take his breath away. He produced a wheezing sound, like a man already inside an oxygen tent. "Are you all right, Zoli?"

"Of course, of course," he said impatiently, leading her toward a pair of tapestry-covered armchairs in a secluded corner. "I still swim my laps in the Lukacs. What else do I need? I'm an old man . . ." He fished a soiled handkerchief out of his trouser pocket and pushed it around his brow. Absent-mindedly, he offered her one of his stubby brown cigarettes and lit one up himself. He inhaled deeply before releasing two streams of dark smoke from his bushy nostrils.

"You are taking risks," she began. "I know things are going on here . . . some of them I can only guess at. But I've already let you down once. I don't really understand what happened to the material. I gave the document to my father. I really don't know what to say. . . ."

"Well, it's possible your father didn't trust the authenticity of the copies," he said. "Or maybe his editors didn't? Who knows? The point is, I trust you. I also need your help, Anna."

"Yes," she said. Believing him absolutely. "I feel . . . strangely . . . that we're on the same side. That's a bizarre twist, isn't it? But, I apologize for this, but I don't quite understand why. After all these years, why you would risk so much now?"

"Listen," he began, his eyes fixed on hers, straining for whatever conviction was left him. "I'm old. I've stood by and let a lot of things happen. Sometimes I've done more than that. I've made them happen. People hauled in. Lives smashed. They never recover, you know. Others driven crazy with fear. Big, smart men who crumbled. Crawled lower than animals. Men of conviction, the most dangerous kind, down on all fours, pleading. While little men . . . of no conviction . . . smiled, and thought it over." He stopped, suddenly out of breath. "I was one of them."

"I don't want to die that way, Anna. I want to repair," he whispered, "what can never be repaired. You know what's at stake now, don't you? The possibility of my country being party to something we understand better than anybody. Occupation. Participating in the rape of a misguided, mismanaged, romantic dream. Soldiers in strange uniforms, our soldiers, taking potshots at frenzied women and crazy kids who won't give up. Just like in '56. Right here. You remember? You were a kid, but you must have a few memories?"

"Yes. Oh, yes," she nodded. "The excitement . . . owning our own country for a few days. And then this crushing letdown. And the soldiers with the strange, oriental faces. From Azerbaijan or someplace, shouting at us, 'Get off the street! Go home!' Only, we *were* home. They looked as afraid of us as we were of them. I remember that much," she said.

"It should not happen again. Not here. Not in Poland." He breathed deeply. "They don't trust me anymore, Anna. I'm finished. This is the work of someone else, someone they haven't caught up with yet." He reached into his inside pocket and produced a small cassette. "He still sits in on important meetings. My friend. This time, Anna," he looked up at her from under his wild nest of a brow, "this time don't let it out of your hands."

She reached for the tape and held onto the old man's

spotted brown hand for just a moment. "Not even Shepherd?" she asked. Knowing he must know. Zoli nodded. "Yes. Shepherd. He's okay."

"You are a brave man," she said, and felt a strange pull. "I will always think of you that way." She wanted to say this now, for she was quite sure she would not have another chance.

"Tell me something, Zoli," she said, both of them already on their feet. "Why did my father do it? The years he worked for the Party? Why?" There was a crack in her voice she hoped he had not heard.

Zoli shook his head. "So your trip was not a success?"

"No," she whispered. "I got no place with him. No place at all."

"Well," he said, "I'm not surprised. How can I explain this to you? He was a Jew." He shrugged. "He had very few options. For a while Laci offered him an option." He turned and walked away from Anna, as if this were not a topic he liked to think or talk about much. And then as he was about to lean against the massive revolving door, he turned slowly and looked at Anna. "There is something else," he said quietly and waited for her to approach. "Those documents. I hoped they would warn him. You see, Alex, like you, has some memories. Only, so many more than you. Memories of '56 and memories of many other things. I had hoped the program for another invasion . . ." he swallowed another rough gulp of air. Anna reached for his arm. "This time with *our* help," Zoli continued, "would warn him . . . this is not the time to come back. . . ."

"My father . . . Come back here?"

"Laci wants him back." Zoli shook his head. "It is hard for you to understand this. In his twisted way, Laci admired your father very much. Trouble is, he needs to humiliate him. To make him small. This is something I recognized the very first time I ever saw the two of them in the same room. This hunger Laci feels to rub out whatever is left of the past . . . the hateful past . . . which Alex, you see, will always remind him of. He can't help it, he reminds Laci where he came from. This is why he got Alex to work for him at a time when, as I told you, Alex had very few offers to consider. But, you see, all the while Laci knew he would never really let him go. The Party rarely does let go. . . ." Zoli dropped his voice to a whisper. "Your father never understood this. Because your father is a relic. He is not from this world. His world does not exist anymore," he said, his face flushed, his voice trembling. "This senseless hate . . . Laci's great gift . . . hate."

"But I don't understand. How can Laci bring him back, if he doesn't want to come?"

"I think that should be rather obvious to you." His voice was under control again, his eyes locked on hers.

"Oh Lord. You mean using me? Why didn't he tell me? I would not have come back then. I would not have risked . . ."

"I don't think that would be your father's style, Anna," Zoli said with a tired smile. "To tell you about something like this? That he was still under some obligation, that he was even remotely tied to a man like Laci. That would be the very last thing he would ever speak to you about. He surely thinks he can work it out with Laci, without you finding out. I hope to God he is right. . . ." Zoli shook his head as he pushed his slow, lumpish body through the revolving doors.

Forty-one

THE ONLY LIGHT IN the television control room came off the blue-gray fluorescent glow of a wall of monitors: incoming feeds from correspondents in Tel Aviv, London, and Managua, and the live soap opera that had begun to roll credits. Technicians, who looked as if they never saw daylight, hunched over the consoles. Hands flipped switches with the confidence of a virtuoso pianist's fingers sliding over a keyboard. The atmosphere in the control room was one of carefully contained tension. It was like this each afternoon, exactly sixty minutes before air time.

"Stand by, Anna," a large man with fifteen years in this room behind him spoke into the snakelike microphone he gripped in his fleshy hand. His voice was dead calm, his cigarette burnt almost down to his index finger. "Five-four-three-two-one. Go, Anna." Anna's grainy image suddenly flashed on three of the monitors. She sat in a Vienna studio, behind her a large map showing the Warsaw Pact countries, Poland encircled in blood red. She spoke slowly and deliberately, anxious for the viewer to seize the weight of her words. This was not just another report from a remote corner of the map. Not that the technicians paid the slightest attention to the meaning of her narrative. They shifted switches and turned knobs to upgrade the quality of the sound and sharpen the picture from the Vienna satellite. That was their job.

Four stories above them, on the network's executive floor, Abe Levin sat in his windowless office, his brows furrowed in concentration. A special monitor connected him to all satellite feeds, which he normally observed with one eye while he continued to conduct business on the telephone. For this feed, however, he sat bolt upright, eyes fixed on the monitor. Her voice had an edge he had never heard before. "UNS News has learned through confidential sources at the highest level of a planned Warsaw Pact invasion and occupation of Poland"—Levin sucked his breath in and held it—"a plan thus far thwarted by an unprecedented split within the ranks of a Warsaw Pact member state, the Hungarian People's Republic. UNS News sources inside the Hungarian Politburo have made available to UNS documents outlining the planned invasion. . . ."

Heavy stuff, Levin thought. Better get her home fast. "Warsaw Pact maneuvers, which have included all Eastern Bloc states with the conspicuous absence of Poland, have been under way for several weeks. According to UNS sources, however, these war games are merely a smokescreen for a very real invasion. Moscow's growing impatience with Warsaw's apparent inability to control civil disobedience, the series of brutal kidnappings of priests and Solidarity leaders, and spiraling economic problems seem to have clinched the Kremlin's decision. In recent weeks, UNS has reported on the editorial campaign launched by Tass and *Izvestia* and picked up by other Warsaw Pact media to prepare the way for this, the tragic resolution of a long-festering problem."

Anna's script, two and one-half minutes long, would lead the evening newscast. More than that, Levin fully expected *The New York Times* and *The Washington Post* to give it banner headlines the next day with attribution to Anna Bator and UNS News. A coup of historic proportions. That, as far as Abe Levin was concerned, was the big story. The prospect of tanks and armored personnel carriers and Soviet, East German, Bulgarian, and possibly, Hungarian divisions streaming across the Polish frontier, well, he'd seen that one before. Levin had been in Hungary in '56 and in Czechoslovakia in '68. It was all on paper, for God's sakes: the Brezhnev Doctrine made it quite plain. It was brutal, heartbreaking even. For the locals, that is.

" . . . It remains to be seen how the rift within the Hungarian Politburo"—Anna was winding up her narration—"will be resolved. And, more importantly, how it will impact on the clear Soviet desire to forge a united front for a military action that will, once again, put all hope of détente in cold storage. This is Anna Bator, UNS News, Vienna, Austria."

"Get me Bator in Vienna," Levin barked into his speakerphone. "Anna. Bravo! You've really done it, sweetheart. No, I won't ask who your source was. Greenwald told me all about the tape. I know you're buttoned up. Listen, it's a hell of a scoop. It's gonna lead the show. We're gonna make the other guys shit. I'm telling you. I knew what I was doing, sending you in there. Heavy-duty stuff. But, listen,

I want you out of there. Better come home now. Get a little
break from all this. I'll get Bradley out of London to stand
by in Vienna. What? You must be kidding! You can't be
serious, Anna. Going back to Budapest is out of the question. Do you hear me? Craziness. Get out of Vienna!" Levin
shouted into the receiver. "Get out of Eastern Europe. This
is not a suggestion, sweetheart. What? You've got two
weeks' vacation coming?" he asked in stunned comprehension "I'm not saying you don't deserve a vacation. But that's
one hell of a place to take a little time off. I don't get it. What
are you trying to prove, Anna? Anna, are you there?"

Forty-two

S HE HAD TO GO BACK. She knew exactly where
on the tape the sound occurred. Over and over, she had
played it, until there was no doubt in her mind. It was hardly
perceptible really, caught between two voices stretched
tight with unspoken tension. Behind the sound of chairs
scraping and throats being cleared. For Anna, the sound was
unmistakable. A cough that was a dry rattle from deep
within his lungs. She had not heard it since her father gave
up smoking after his first heart attack, five years ago. He
must have picked up his old habit again. The cough, whose
unmistakable sound used to announce his presence, had
returned. Her father was in Budapest. Her father had sat in
on a meeting to discuss the fate of Poland.

So she had to come back. The idea of returning to the
security of New York while her father was in Budapest was
unthinkable.

Sure, there were risks involved. But her passport and
Shepherd's presence in the city gave her this absurd feeling
of being inviolable.

She had not yet finished unpacking her suitcase, back in her old room at the Hilton, when the phone rang.

"Hello," she said brightly. "You sound too remote. Are you on a provincial boondoggle somewhere?"

"No. I'm in Vienna," Shepherd answered, his voice flat. "Where I expected to find you."

"Chris, I had to come back. Something important . . ."

"I needn't tell you what sort of tempest you've stirred up . . ."

"Don't tell me any of that. Tell me when you're coming home. And how much you've missed me."

"Darling, you haven't heard? I'm not coming back," he said in a deliberate monotone. "I can't. They've declared me persona non grata."

"Oh my God."

"I had forty-eight hours to pack and leave. I can't tell you what I felt, as I drove across the border. Maybe for the last time. I still can't believe it," he said, his control beginning to slip.

"But . . . but why?" she asked uselessly.

"They told me I was lucky. Getting off easy. The tape. It hit them where it hurts, Anna. Your little two-and-a-half-minute spot."

Anna fell silent, struck by her own naivete. The armor of the Western reporter.

"Anna, are you there, sweetheart?"

"Yes," she whispered. "Yes, I'm here. I feel cold." She wondered if this was how her mother felt, chatting on the phone, while four men slowly climbed the stairs. "Scared stiff, if you want to know the truth."

"Darling. I'm so sorry not to be there. But you must

leave. You must." He hissed the last two words. Inflated them with his frustration and fear. "You must," he repeated once more. And then they both heard a long, low whine on the line which blew away each other's voices.

Anna sat on the too-large hotel bed, her hands limp in her lap. And waited. She wondered then how she had come to this hotel room, and to this waiting. Why was she not in her New York apartment, reading a bedtime story to Sarah, with her handsome, imperfect husband in the next room? But no, even while she thought this, she knew that scenario had not been feasible, given her circumstances.

She did not have her parents' fear. A protective, primal layer of fear had enabled them to accomplish so much: deny the past, lie even to their child. They could even slip into new identities. All this made possible by a fear Anna did not possess. Without it, the bargain they had struck didn't work. Anna had not been a party to the deal they had made with themselves and their circumstance. She had rejected her inheritance.

At some point, as all the morality plays point out, someone has to start paying up; untangling the circles of deletions and deceptions. And so she sat there, afraid to move, and listened for a knock.

Forty-three

ONCE A WEEK, they allowed her to select two books from the musty, windowless room with the steel gray shelving that served as the prison library. She was working her way through a nearly complete set of Dickens. She savored the uncompromising morality and the Victorian bulk of his prose.

Even *Little Dorrit*. Once, her father had written to her from this place, "You must read Dickens." She understood now why Dickens. It was good prison reading, suitable for a reader with endless time to kill.

What had they told Sarah? "Mommy will be home soon, darling. You must be good so she'll be proud of you when she comes home." Soon. They had told Anna the same thing. Did Sarah know what prison meant? She hoped not. Had they all forgotten her? What the hell was the embassy doing?

Though the dead air of her cell was ill suited for this purpose, she breathed a deep, cleansing breath. The calming breathing she had learned for natural childbirth. Oh, Sarah.

How long had it been? Twenty-three days and two hours. She had learned to tell prison time, from the grimy rays of light the barred, screened window allowed and from the guards' movements. It was nine-thirty in the morning, three hours since they handed her the tin mug and the dark bread which she devoured crumb by crumb. In the morning, it was fresh. Another half hour until the matron, who still refused to acknowledge Anna's obstinate smile, led her to the prison yard. Twenty minutes of up and down, up and down, never look up at the sky. She had learned to defy this most perverse of the many laws governing the prisoner's life. She sneaked stealthy looks up, knew when it was blue, gray, or streaked pink. Sarah's sky.

The nights were the hardest. Endless and perfectly lonely, at night Anna often forgot to hope. This morning, she awoke to find warm dribbles of sweat streaked from her hair down her cheeks. Again, the dream of the light steps behind her. Her legs growing thicker, slower, slower. Unable, finally, to move at all. Stuck in some invisible mud. A blurred face closing in on her, coming into focus, "Come, Anna." The face, so desiccated it looked almost like a death's head. A dead face. Laci's face. Laci's skeletal hands on the chubby arms of the little girl in a black pinafore. Leading her toward a misty place where others already stood and waited in orderly lines.

She rose from her cot. How had her mother and father coped? Those weeks and months in here. She no longer had dreams about her father. She supposed because she spent so many of her waking hours thinking about him. She was beginning to understand certain things about him. She was learning about fear.

Her father had not crumbled under far worse pressures than Anna's. She knew nothing about the hot stab of pain from a cigarette brushed "carelessly" against your cheek. Or the shock of a hard fist which tires of pounding the table, and seeks a softer target. Still her father had resisted putting his name to a phony confession. Until they offered him something in return. A trip out of here forever. A ticket to a new life on the other side of the world. But at what price.

She would do anything now to see her little girl. Anything at all.

"This way, 3844." The guard stuck his head into the cell. Down the long, carpeted (not for comfort, but for absolute quiet) corridor, he led her to the elevator. They never told her where they were taking her. They lurched down four or five flights in an elevator without buttons or numbers for floors. She recognized the office. The pink geraniums in the window looked brighter than ever. In fact, the whole office looked cheerful to her. It had real chairs, not just a cot. And a shiny desk of real wood. Major Berci Toth sat behind it and did not acknowledge Anna's presence.

"How many times did you see the American, Shepherd?" he asked without looking up. They had covered this ground before. Her answers did not improve with practice. She had learned that they really weren't after her answers so much as a certain state of indifference on her part. They wanted her in a soft place where she no longer cared about lines between truth and lies, where her only emotion was a profound desire to put an end to all of this.

"Many times. I have no exact number. We were friends," she repeated. Berci scowled at that word, as though he would have to look it up in his dictionary.

"What is it about you Jews?" he asked, rubbing his cleft chin one large index finger. Anna had never been called a Jew in her life. It had a strange, and, in his mouth, a poisonous sound. "Why do you always have to meddle in other people's business?"

"What has that got to do with anything?" she asked, revulsion momentarily overcoming her better judgment to stay quiet. Hot little pinpricks of anger and fear shot through her temples, her palms.

"Everything. It's always been like that here. This is a small country. We notice who's what. Maybe it was different, over there?"

"Yes," she answered softly, "it was different over there."

"Whatever the case, you are going to be charged under Section I, Article 70, of the Criminal Code of the People's Republic with espionage for the Imperialists," he announced with cool professionalism.

Anna remembered that number, that code. For an instant, the remarkable symmetry between her parents' case and her own blurred any other reaction.

"You haven't got the right"; she breathed deeply, willed her voice to stay level. "I am an American citizen. Protected by my country's laws."

"I must say, they've been pretty quiet about your case," he said. "Hardly a peep out of 'your country.' " He pronounced this with such sardonic satisfaction, she began to think maybe she had been forgotten, left to rot in the Fo Street, for the sake of "global" concerns. Then she remembered: This was precisely their intention, to isolate the prisoner, make him feel alone. She pulled herself up in her chair, looked him straight in the eye, and said nothing.

"All right, you can go back to your cell now," he said scornfully. "Your lack of cooperative spirit has not escaped notice at the highest levels."

Laci, she thought, and smiled.

Forty-four

THE HEAVY DOOR was pushed open by so deft a hand she hardly heard him come in. He was already standing in front of her when she looked up. A spare, towering wreck of a man, radiating almost unbearable melancholy. He had looked this way that day in the school yard, awaiting his trial.

"Papa," she sobbed, as she had then. She flung herself against the familiar feel of good cotton, the smell of English cigarettes and Eau de Cologne. Just then, he seemed restored to his full size. She wanted him full size. She herself had been made so small by prison. She loved him excruciatingly. He must have come to take her home. She would be his little girl again, unquestioning and keenly aware of her good fortune.

He sat down on her cot with his familiar grace, as though it were a settee. She straightened up from her slump. He did not speak. They sat there for what seemed like long moments, in stunned silence, thinking their own thoughts.

He avoided looking at his daughter, as shocked by her appearance as she had once been by his.

"You and I next to each other on a cot in the Fo Street." She shook her head in disbelief. His features were set in an expression of unspeakable sadness.

"Anna"—he breathed deeply, finally—"you should not have done this." His tone was drenched with blame. She felt her chosen role slip away. The trusting child did not exist any longer. She looked fiercely at his tired eyes, the same eyes she used to bait for approval, affection, and esteem. She would have given anything to have that superior, just-beyond-her-reach father of hers back. He had taught her to expect so much from him. Let her assume so many things. But he was gone.

"Why did you come back?" he asked, his voice as tight as a violin's strings. "Why on earth did you walk back in here after Vienna?" She understood from his tone he had not come to free her. The knot of fear, like a fist, hardened in her stomach.

"I *had* to. Don't you see? I heard you. I heard your cough on the tape. It *was* you. Now I know for sure. I wouldn't have otherwise. I would never have known for sure."

He sighed deeply. "My cough," he said in stunned comprehension, and made a sound like a snort. A short, dry, unmistakable message. That, once again, life had played a dirty trick on him. Then she knew that her father had vanished in the mists of her own childhood. Or worse still, he had never existed at all. She had an urge to cry out, "It's not true!"

"Anna," he said, running his long fingers through his thin, gray hair. "My life . . ." he paused, unaccustomed to talking about his life to his child or anyone else. "My life . . . has been a failure." He stared at the ground. "It should not have been. But that is the way it has evolved." He looked up at her with such pain in his eyes, she looked away. "For you," he said, "I wanted something different. And we came so close. . . ."

"But it didn't work," she said. "You see now, don't you? What you tried to do could not work?"

"Why not?" he asked, frustration and anger pitching his voice higher. "Have you ever seen a refugee who looks less like a refugee? Yes, even now . . . here in this damned place. Or sounds less like a refugee? You have everything, Anna. Debt-free. It was all for you. . . ."

"Yes. I was a little bit of everything. So, nothing . . . No connection between my early memories and the present. Or between you and me. Not really. Like two separate lives carefully sealed off from each other. So I had nothing to push away from—and eventually come back to. Children need that to grow up. I never really grew up. I was floating in this unreal place you made up for me. Now I know I am an American. I mean, you have to know what you are—or were—before you can call yourself that." As she said this she was struck by its simple truth. "Yes," she said, "don't you see? I've earned my identity now."

He said nothing, his head like a great weight held in both hands.

"I'm not saying you ought to profess to be something you do not believe in," she went on. "Only that you should have made that choice available to me. It is a terrible thing, to find out about yourself from others, from strangers. And something else," she paused, knowing this would hurt, "you should *not* have made me think of you as someone who is not afraid . . . not afraid to stand up for . . . for things that are not easy to stand up for . . . not afraid to be alone. When, all along, you *have* been afraid. Not so much for your life, but afraid of what you were."

"I'm sorry," he said in a broken voice, "that you did not know me . . . before . . . before things went bad. My good years," he forced a smile, "were very short."

She felt sorry for both of them. A tide of warmth washed over her for this beaten man. She had never felt more love for him than in their mutual loss. She was not the daughter he hoped for. He was far from the father she needed. Could they start from those modest expectations? Now?

"What has happened to Poland?" she asked, searching for an escape from their pain. "The invasion?"

"It did not take place. Their surprise was spoiled. Congratulations," he said with an ironic smile.

She would have liked to have taken pleasure at this news. To have felt proud of her role in it. But just then, she could not.

"You have not come to take me home," she said. "Have you?"

"Yes . . . maybe," he said, again looking down at the hard floor. "You are free to go. Under certain circumstances. They have asked me to propose this to you. . . ." He still did not look up. "You are free to go, Anna, if you will, from time to time, be available for . . . for sort of freelance work. File stories that will . . . on occasion . . . suit their needs. Help them . . . in small ways. . . ." His voice faded away.

"How could you?" she asked, electric with the shock of this. "From father to daughter! They want to own me too?" She heard her own voice rising. "No! Tell Laci I *will not*. I have a child. I do not want her to find out things when she grows up that I could not tell her myself. Tell Laci," she said, high on a wave of determination coming from an unexpected place, "tell him I prefer to stay where I am." Her hate had taken its own course. It spared her of a decision. For Laci, who once forced a hideous choice upon her father, she would do nothing.

Her father rose slowly from the cot, his shoulders hunched. He seemed to draw his body into itself. She wanted him gone, so she would not have time to reconsider. But he did not push. That was not his style. She heard his soft knock on the door, heard the guard's key and the door close behind him.

Forty-five

"Y OU ARE going to be released." Major Toth
looked down at Anna, whose copy of *The Pickwick Papers*
slipped from her lap and landed on the floor with a crash.
"You can collect your things, your jewelry, money, whatever, after you've washed and fixed up," he said, looking
with distaste at her tangled hair. She continued to stare at
him with round, unblinking eyes.

"The Summit. The one they've been talking about so
long nobody believed it would happen. Well, it's about to
happen. In Geneva. Reagan and Gorbachev," he said, for she
had still not reacted or responded. "So everybody is doing
a little house cleaning. Sprucing up. Setting the stage for a
few weeks of good feeling. You are very lucky."

Geneva, she thought. Again Geneva. A Summit. Well,
we are little people, serving big events in small ways. Suddenly, she was overwhelmed by a pulsing happiness. Sarah.
I will see Sarah. A warm current raced through her body
like a life-saving drug. An unbearable, lightheaded joy seized
her. She jumped to her feet.

"I shall see my daughter."

"Yes," he said, rapping softly on the door. "Yes. They've arranged for her to come and see you. We shall keep your passport, you see." He cleared his throat unnecessarily. "They have decided that the . . . ah . . . the way you left . . . with your father and mother was not quite *acceptable.* So," he said matter-of-factly, "you are now, once again, a Hungarian citizen. Your daughter can come and go as she likes," he concluded with a smile, as though breaking good news.

"I don't understand," she had been trying to follow his words. "What do you mean? I am American. I have a U.S. passport."

"Not any more," he shook his head. "It's gone. Official property. Confiscated. You left illegally to begin with. But you are free to live wherever you choose, in your own country." He turned his back and was gone. Anna was left in the guard's care. In a trance she followed him to the showers. Blindly, she slipped off the green silk blouse and linen skirt, wrinkled and soiled beyond recognition. Her head was spinning as she washed herself, but she tried not to think about the future yet. I shall soon hold Sarah, she thought. Out of here.

Then, it occurred to her that her father must be in trouble. If their officially sanctioned "escape" had been declared null and void, something had happened to him.

She was free. Free to leave the Fo Street, at least. After eighty-five days and nights in that dark, hopeless world, she was walking out. Beyond that, she could not think.

Forty-six

D ID I REALLY THINK this a drab place once? I walked out of the Fo Street dazzled by the light and the colors of the city. Budapest offered up its ancient magic. How is it I never before marveled at the houses of jonquil yellow and ripe orange that blend together to create a Cézanne landscape out of Buda's lush, rolling hills? I inhaled the heady summertime smells of freshly cut grass and the chestnut trees that drooped with their growth. Everywhere people sat aimlessly in outdoor cafés. The smell of good coffee and suntan-oiled bodies was almost more than I could bear. Like a long-interned patient suddenly released from the hospital, my legs felt liquid under me, but I was anxious to touch and smell and feel every new thing.

Sarah turned out to have amazingly acute instincts. We have grown particularly close. Each night, I wait to hear the scrape of her pajama feet against the bare floor as she stumbles from her bed to mine. "Just a snuggle, Mommy," she says, but stays till morning. She goes back to New York in the fall. She will come again at midterm. Sam has been more

than generous in financing her travels. I suppose I see her
nearly as much as many other divorced parents see their kids
these days. But this is not what I had in mind.

Our life is modest. We have found a two-room apartment, badly in need of paint, with a dingy kitchen, in a villa
on the Hill of Roses. It isn't far from Christopher's old place.
Each morning, I fill a string bag with our needs for the day
at the open market on Moscow Square. Thanks mostly to
Sarah's open, uninhibited personality, we have made a few
friends. Memories of pushing a heaping cart around the
gleaming aisles of an ice-cold supermarket, making choices
that would now boggle my mind, are already growing dim.

I've stopped having those dreams. Perhaps, once you
confront in real life the characters who people your dreams,
you destroy their power over you. What more can Laci do
to me now? I'm no threat to anybody. UNS News has
stopped protesting to the Hungarian government. So has
the State Department. I'm not really surprised by their short
attention span. There are too many other things going on
in Washington and New York.

I've finally stopped picking away at old wounds. I accept
now that my father loves me, as much as he can manage. His
life is his. Mine is mine. We are both much reduced, but
strangely at peace. Both with each other and our circumstances. I'm not recommending it as a solution to anybody's
problems, but prison does seem to boil things down to their
essential parts. Like an illness, I suppose. In a very short
time, I made certain discoveries about myself; what is nego-
tiable for me and what is not, things I never would have
understood in my former life. If only the price extracted for
the year's truths had not been so high.

I also seem to have developed a finer sense for small

things. I notice the swoop of a gull as it skims the Danube, or a leaf fluttering slowly to the ground. Small, insular countries have this benefit: they help sharpen your perceptions. There are far fewer distractions here.

I still don't know what sort of an agreement Laci, his old comrade and nemesis, and my father reached. But this is one of the very few things about him I don't know. The point is the Party has reclaimed my father as it has now claimed me. We see each other only about once a month, as he lives in the northeastern town of Debrecen. He makes a bare living teaching English at the Calvinist University there. He says he spends his evenings translating Galsworthy into Hungarian: *The Forsyte Saga*, a book with special meaning for him. I can't imagine this is what Laci had in mind when he forced him to return from New York, using me as bait.

My father's life, like mine, is in a very minor key these days, of little consequence to anybody. Yet he does not sound bitter or angry. I think he has looked his ghosts in the eye, too. He has nothing left to hide or fear. Neither from me nor from them.

"You see," he said to me the last time we were together, "things *have* changed here. In the old days you and I would never be allowed to live like this . . . in such freedom. Not after . . . so many things." He means what I did to Laci. My television report which broke the planned Warsaw Pact invasion of Poland would have earned me permanent oblivion not so long ago. And my father along with me.

"This is really a beautiful country," he said, as though discovering it for the first time. "I will take you to Kecskemét after Sarah leaves you. I found the most sensational Art Nouveau architecture . . . I never knew it existed."

"I'd like that," I answer.

Forty-seven

I N THE EVENING, just as I am tucking Sarah in for
the night, the telephone rings. "Hello, Anna," the familiar,
resonant voice breaks over the transatlantic line.

"Christopher." I don't want to cry. I want him to think
of me as stronger than I am. "Christopher," I repeat. I love
the sound of his name and hear it so rarely now.

"Anna. I love you, Anna."

"I love you too, Christopher . . . I miss you terribly. Why
didn't we talk more when we had the chance? That's what
keeps me awake at night, you know. How much we didn't
say."

"Yes," he says and pauses. "I liked kissing you too
much." Neither of us regards these weekly calls as private.
"I am still waiting for my posting. I hope it won't be too far
from Hungary. Washington is unbearable in August. Much
less nice than Budapest."

"I remember." But I barely do.

"It will be all right. Things change, you know." He says
this every week. I can feel his pain as sharply as my own.

I have a feeling we shall love each other for a very long time. It was always different before, with Sam and the others. This is almost like a timeless friendship. It's not possible for us to stop loving each other.

"I'll never stop hoping."

And we hung up. What is there to say?

Sarah and I took a rickety old train to Visegrád two weeks ago. Zoli was buried in the town where he spent the last six months of his life, in enforced retirement. How he must have missed his dips in the Lukacs. And the cafés. I'm glad we went. Only a small handful of people were there to see his coffin lowered into the ground. They all resembled him. Wrinkled and sagging, but with sharp, intelligent eyes. At least they allowed him to live out his days a more or less free man. My father is right; things have changed.

I haven't got the temperament for despair. I still look forward to certain things. Someday, I will tell Sarah the story of how when I was an American television reporter I helped to foil the surprise invasion of one of our neighboring countries. I look forward to answering her questions about her parents, her grandparents, and her great-grandparents. With this rich inheritance, Sarah will never feel like an exile in her own country. Some families take longer to get it right than others.

There is no electricity in my life now. Not the sort of wild excitement I used to feel when I approached the lights and cameras, radioactive with a big story. There are still unexpected little moments, though, which make my blood pump a bit faster, moments which miraculously escape the long reach of history or politics. For instance, yesterday, riding in the subway, I was aware of a pair of deep brown eyes fixed unselfconsciously on me as I pretended to read a paperback. Those eyes felt nice and warm. Life still offers small, unexpected turns.

Sarah and I walk slowly along the Danube promenade each evening when the sky abruptly turns a deep hyacinth. The city looks particularly soft and seductive. Too innocent for a memory. But I feel as though I have become the collective memory of the Bator family. I remember things that happened before my birth. I remember Barcelona 1936. Budapest and Kistarcsa 1944. New York. It is all part of me now. I also wait for better times, an American trait.

I fill every corner of my lungs with that lush, late August night air. I cannot seem to get enough of this. "Tighter," Sarah commands me to squeeze her chubby hand. She has not forgotten our time apart. Nor have I. I squeeze her hand until she says, "Ouch!" And we both laugh. Strangers who pass and mistake this for real happiness smile at us.